TRANSCENDENCE
CALLING

TRANSCENDENCE
CALLING

The Power of Kundalini Rising and Spiritual Enlightenment

Monique Rebelle

ENKAI Publishing
Reno, Nevada

Publisher's Cataloging-in-Publication data

Names: Rebelle, Monique, author.
Title: Transcendence calling : the power of kundalini rising and spiritual enlightenment / Monique Rebelle.
Description: Reno, NV: ENKAI Publishing, 2018.
Identifiers: ISBN 978-0-692-98553-3
Subjects: LCSH Rebelle, Monique. | Artists--Biography. | Spiritual biography. | Kundalini. | Chakras. | Mind and body. | BISAC BODY, MIND & SPIRIT / Inspiration & Personal Growth | BODY, MIND & SPIRIT / New Thought | BODY, MIND & SPIRIT / Mysticism
Classification: LCC BL73 .R43 2018 | DDC 204/.36092--dc23

Front cover image:

"Fire Goddess" by Monique Rebelle oil on canvas 60x72"
Painted on Maui, Hawaii, two months after the spontaneous kundalini rising, Fire Goddess is the equivalent of Kundalini Shakti known as the divine spiritual power within every human being.

Illustrations:

"Kundalini ascending through the dimensions of perception (chakras)."
Monique Rebelle, oil on canvas 24X30".

Printed in the United States of America

First Printing, 2018
Cover design: Deana Riddle, Monique Rebelle
Interior design: Deana Riddle, Monique Rebelle
Author's photo: Peter Walker Photography

 ENKAI Publishing
1690 Murphy Pl.
Reno, Nevada 89521

Ordering Information:
Quantity sales: Special discounts are available on bulk purchases. For details, contact the author at info@moniquerebelle.com

"We are all on this planet together. We are all brothers and sisters with the same physical and mental faculties, the same problems, and the same needs. We must all contribute to the fulfillment of the human potential and the improvement of the quality of life as much as we are able. Mankind is crying for our help. Ours is a desperate time. Those who have something to offer should come forward. Now is the time."

His Holiness The 14th Dalai Lama

I am very thankful and grateful to those who helped me with the process of creating this book:

Anna Krystyna Gawrońska – whose enthusiasm and dedication got this project going, Dominika Szaciłło, Haley Anderson, Bruce Hollihan, Scott Ewers, Deana Riddle, Martha Bullen, Lucetta Zaytoun, Joshua Gibbs, Dan Gunnarson, Mary Ann Fernandez, Peter Frank, Barry Bruninga, Tamra Fleming, Bill Collins, Deanna Ford, Bradley Carlson, and Christopher Hill.

For my awesome daughter - Dominika

mama

CONTENTS

INTRODUCTION

Why Did I Write This Book?

My experience happened spontaneously in 1992. I hoped to put it into words one day and share it with anyone who was interested, but for years I did not feel ready to take that step. While I contemplated writing this book, several others who underwent the same experience shared descriptions of their own awakenings, some became spiritual teachers. Although the results of these experiences are ultimately the same, the journey often varies greatly from person to person. In hopes of the best possible understanding of this sublime phenomenon, I knew that I would have to open myself up and reveal the intimate details of the most sacred time of my life. I am usually a direct and, sometimes, a foolishly outspoken person, but I can also be quite private when it comes to my personal life. This time I had to let go of my secrets and accept an uneasy level of vulnerability and exposure.

Another issue that has held me back from writing this book sooner, is the fact that I've never had ambitions to be a teacher. As an independent, free-spirited individual, I didn't think it was necessary to give anyone a recipe for life. However, since I now know, without a doubt, that every person has the potential to have the same experience, contributing my findings may be helpful, especially because the journey toward such an experience can be very difficult. When I first attempted to describe what happened, I simply could not find words to express it. I had no prior knowledge of anything like it and the depth and expansiveness of the revealed state seemed simply impossible to explain. Still, even without putting it into words, I knew exactly what had happened and remembered everything down to the smallest detail – I "got it", forever.

In time, as I came to grips with this transformational experience in a more tangible way, I was able to create a basic description of the process that I had undergone. After a little longer, I had compiled enough comparisons with the obtainable data that I could place my description into the context of already available information and present it from that viewpoint as well. Finally, I gave up trying to be a perfectionist and holding on to the unworkable idea of describing all my realizations connected with the experience. This allowed me to be much more at peace with the whole endeavor. I did eventually become a spiritual teacher and the sharing of my experience has become a mutual learning process. While I offer support on the path to self-realization, my students teach me how to communicate in a way that relates directly to their life and their needs.

It is my hope that I can explain my experience clearly to help you gain more power on your own path. However, no matter how skillfully I describe what I went through, the magnitude of it is still minimized by words; nothing can reveal it in its totality. The only way to really know it is to experience it oneself and I hope this book will be a motivating force towards self-realization. It appears to me that while literature that explores the subject of the subtle body, chakras, and associated practices aimed at leading one to a spiritual awakening is quite in depth, the information about the final results of those practices may seem limited in comparison. Conversely, descriptions by people who had full, spontaneous experiences are usually written with less interest in process and are more about the results of those experiences. It is my aim to show both aspects of the phenomena - a subjective look into a spontaneous occurrence in an unsuspecting individual and also a report on an event understood by humanity as one that leads to spiritual enlightenment. It is my desire that this will make the information more accessible, understandable, and relatable to all who read it.

This book consists of three major parts:

1. My Life Before the Experience

To some, my story may seem very dramatic and unique. To others, it won't seem as extreme or as difficult as their own experiences or as the fates of other people they've heard about. I do not strive to prove that unusual or extraordinary life circumstances are necessary to experience the depth of our consciousness; rather, I hope to convey that something very important can be learned from the way our lives unfold. Each person can find a link to direct spiritual enlightenment, regardless of their life path.

The reason I was at first reluctant to write about my past is because after self-realization, we no longer see our existence the same way. We don't feel the same way about our lives and we don't think about them as we used to. One's personal story is not as significant anymore, because it becomes clear that whatever happened before was there for one reason: to lead one to a new state of being.

I also realized that in order to be understood, I needed to present the context in which my experience took place and to explain what kind of person I was before it happened. Thus, I provide information about some of the events that, in my opinion, were the factors leading to my experience in 1992. Most of them occurred during my childhood and youth and they influenced the decisions I've made throughout my life, for good or bad, whether I was aware of it or not.

2. The Experience

This part is divided into two chapters. In the first, I describe the experience, with as much clarity as possible. At this point, I do not offer further explanations based on preexisting knowledge about the phenomenon. At the time, I had never heard the word kundalini, nor did I believe in chakras. I did not even consider spiritual enlightenment to be a real thing. I lived through it without any conscious preparation. The download of information during the experience was much more rich and profound than I could ever define in words; therefore, in this part, I focus on the general sequence of events and their meaning, as I was able to grasp it. My purpose is to describe a process that is universal, although not yet commonly attended.

The second section is dedicated to the basic, most significant changes in my life caused by the experience. It is a report of a personal journey, with the turning point marking the beginning of a new person who was freed from the past, infused with divine energy, and changed forever.

3. Seven Worlds - One Truth

In this part I offer comprehensive explanation of the experience based on comparisons with already established information (purposefully limited - to keep my own experience independently alive). My knowledge, in many instances, aligns with what is already known, but I also share new insights and introduce a new approach to both general and particular elements of the phenomena of kundalini rising and spiritual enlightenment. This new system emerges directly from the study of my own experience and conclusions reached by in-depth investigation since the experience. I present practices that can be applied in one's life in order to proceed on a solid, natural spiritual path without the religious doctrine.

The last chapter in this part of the book is dedicated to questions and answers taken from sessions with my students.

PART ONE:

Life

CHAPTER I: MY LIFE BEFORE THE EXPERIENCE

Childhood and Youth in Poland

I was born in Warsaw, Poland, a child of professional actors. My mother did not want children and my parents were just about to separate when she discovered she was over four months pregnant. A nurse who looked after theater kids took care of me for the first year of my life. After a year with the nurse, I moved in with my grandmother in a little town close to Warsaw and lived with her for the next three years. While my grandmother taught in the local high school I remained under the supervision of various maids. I had no siblings and being alone was something that I was used to and thought nothing of, it was fine. Later, we moved to Warsaw to join my mother. She had divorced my father and he had moved out of town to become a theater director in northern Poland. I grew up without him. My grandmother passed away when I was 12 years old. My mother remarried a year later, and soon after, we moved to a better apartment in the center of Warsaw. I graduated from high school with the intention of studying painting at the Warsaw Academy of Fine Arts, but that never happened. Instead, I left Poland when I was 19 years old.

Childhood Events

Several episodes from my childhood prompted me to make specific decisions early on. As much as I could, I tried to act on those decisions. I could focus on myself because my early childhood was generally quite uneventful, and I could just sit and think as much as I wanted. Internally, I nursed an exciting vision of my future, but I never talked to anyone about it.

I was about two and a half years old, when one day, while I was playing with some toys in my room, my grandma walked in. She sat in a chair by the wall, some distance from me, and after some time she suddenly said, "And they split up", then she began to cry. At first, I was not sure who she was talking about, but eventually I guessed she was referring to my parents. It puzzled me to see her weeping, but she soon got up and left my room. I felt disturbed by that event and spent some time thinking about it. Lying in bed that evening, I could not fall asleep and wondered why people would get together in the first place if they would only separate later. I felt the pain of separation, and it bothered me. I decided then that rather than risking a breakup, I would just live life on my own, but that also made me nervous. "Don't people live together for a reason? How will I do by myself?" my 30-month-old mind questioned. I could not figure it out, so, for the first time I made the decision to remember the question and come back to it later, after I'd gained enough knowledge to answer it.

I noticed my mother said several times on different occasions, "poor child," about me, especially when she thought I was sleeping. Once, I opened my eyes and asked "Why?", but she offered me no answer. It felt good to have something to do with my question - it went straight to the "memory box".

My grandmother lived through WWI in France, the Bolshevik Revolution in Moscow, and WWII in Poland. She endured a lot and was separated from her family and loved ones more than once, yet she maintained a positive outlook and was quite often enthusiastic about life. She was talented, spoke seven languages, sang, played piano, and was an excellent visual artist. I was about 3 years old when she began teaching me to play the piano and to sing. We had a couple of lessons and it was a lot of fun. We sang in French. One day, my mother arrived from Warsaw while we were in the middle of a piano lesson. She was displeased by what she saw and told my grandmother that she did not want me to learn music. I could see my grandmother was upset and I could feel she did not agree, but respected my mother's decision. From then on, I was not allowed to play the piano or sing. I did not know what to think; I only knew my mother was the ultimate authority so there was no further discussion.

Another event I remember well was a punishment I received when I was 3 years old. I was given a toy wheelbarrow as a gift. I was so excited! For some reason, putting things in a wheelbarrow and pushing it around the room made me happy. Excited, I went outside the house, into our fenced yard. I tried to push the toy on a sandy path and then on the grass but it was not working well. I realized that a harder and smoother surface was needed. The paved sidewalk was right outside the gate, and even though I'd never gone there on my own, I knew how to open the gate, and I did not recall anybody forbidding me from passing through. I pushed my new wheelbarrow down the sidewalk with passion, but it didn't last long before I was caught and brought back home. It turned out I was not allowed to go outside of the yard. My mother grabbed our dog's leash and beat me. I had no time to explain the reasons behind my actions. I did not even know that what I had done was "wrong". She assumed I knew, but that I was just being disobedient. The beating hurt me very bad; I could not believe how painful it was. I also felt very hurt emotionally because it was so unfair. The next day I was still shaken up and confused. Our dog, a dachshund, was a very sweet and friendly pet. I remember holding his leash in my hand and starting to beat him with it. In a compulsive reaction to what was done to me, I wanted to feel power over something, and execute it. Instantly, after the first lashes he squirmed in pain, tied to the leash I was holding, unable to run away. I watched his pain in shock and I abruptly stopped what I was doing. Thoughts ran through my mind and culminated in a firm decision: "No! This is horrible. From now on, I am not going to hurt anything."

When I was about 4 years old, grandma informed me that we would be moving to Warsaw to be with my mother. I did not want to go. I was happy where I was and preferred to let things stay as they were. "It is important for you to be with your mother," my grandma said. I trusted her. Despite initial doubts, I was easily convinced that the transition would ultimately be good for me, and I accepted it.

As soon as we moved to Warsaw, theater entered my life. My mother would take me to work with her and I could watch the plays from behind the curtains and watch my mother getting ready to go on stage. I told myself that I would like to be like her when I grew up.

There were actors all around and they were always very nice to me. They often talked to me, already in their costumes, before going on stage or after coming off it, their pronunciation so exact, their voices distinguished and beautiful. Completely taken by their attention I was too shy to talk... I fell in love with theater and could not wait to go there again.

"Starstruck, I watched this ravishing woman perform and boundless admiration would fill me up every time."

I remember wandering around in the audience hall, still empty before the afternoon performance, and thinking about how much I loved theater, and how I was ready to spend my life in theater myself. The stage felt like the most desirable place to be, my real home, because that's where I knew my parents were. When I watched the shows, I could emotionally tune in and live through the ups and downs of the dramatic plots. The drama onstage brought me fulfillment, even as I watched the same performances time and time again. Seeing my mother on stage was a showstopper for me. Starstruck, I watched this ravishing woman perform and boundless admiration would fill me up every time. Oh, I cherished my sweet secret: she was *not* Diana from *Little Red Hood* - she was *my mother!*

I loved my mother and would seek her approval whenever I could. When I was about 6 years old, my father sent me some clothing as a gift. This angered my mother, "No more gifts," she said firmly. My grandmother objected, claiming the gifts had nothing to do with my mother's relationship with her ex-husband but were for me and I should be allowed to receive them. I jumped right to my mother's defense with, "I don't need any gifts." I remember being surprised by my own behavior.

One day, when I was 7 years old, my mother told me I was not allowed to go to the theater with her anymore. Her friend, who was visiting at that time, was surprised by the statement and asked my mother why. "She might like it too much," my mother said testily. As soon as I learned I would not be able to go to theater, I felt a heavy weight descending on me and my knees got weak. My mother's verdict hit me hard. I instinctively grabbed the side of a bookshelf and hid behind it to regain my composure. Theater was so important in my life. I had built a wonderful world around it and saw it as my future. I was crushed, but I was aware nothing would change my mother's resolution and I had to live with it.

Overall though, life was going relatively smoothly; I liked school, I had good friends, and plenty of enthusiastic energy. I had to accept that my mother would not allow me to study music in school, but I could take drawing classes. It was fun. Whenever I was home, if I was not doing my homework, I was sitting in my room drawing.

My grandma got ill and passed away some months later. During the last two years of her life, she was barely present; she talked to people who were not in the room and, at the end, I was not even sure she knew who I was. I was shocked when I heard that she had died and deeply sorry that I had no chance to say goodbye.

I always tried to find justification for my mother's decisions, so I could agree with her and feel at peace with what was going on. After all, people were always saying, "Mother knows best," and that it was obvious that she loved me. One time, preparing for our school assignment, a paper titled "My Mother's Love", I felt a need to ask if she really loved me, because she never said it. "To love you one needs to understand you" my mother said grandly; the facial expression which followed, showed her usual exasperation, as if she wanted to say I should have known that instead of bothering her. I felt bad, but I could not recall my mother ever asking me to explain something she did not understand about me. It was a completely new issue I knew nothing about, but I still felt guilty for not being understood by her. I did not use her statement in my school paper but kept it for myself stashed in the "memory box" to be figured out later.

When she laughed me off after I told her I wanted to take dance lessons, there was nothing I could say back. She simply said, "You do not look good enough to be a dancer." I figured she had to know best, since I was only 12 and she was an experienced professional. All along, I secretly waited for my father to come and take me out of my mother's hands.

When I was 13 years old, my mother remarried. She did not tell me she was getting married and I did not know anything about the wedding. One day, when I entered my mother's room I was surprised to find masses of flowers all over the place. Her new husband was in the room at that time and I asked him about the flowers. He thought I was being mean by ignoring their big day.

Life in Poland was equally confusing for me. In school, we were supposed to worship the October Revolution and Lenin, but the history we were being taught in school was different from what I was told at home. By the time I was 14, I was certain that people hated the system but were forced to pretend otherwise.

At the end of my first year of high school, I was chosen to play the lead in a school play. When my mother found out about the performance, she looked at me as if I'd committed a serious crime. The production was very successful, everybody in school was excited about it, and there was even a mention in the local paper, but at home, I was shunned for it. I was given a lecture on how all actresses were unhappy and how stupid it was for me to want to be one. Eventually, she managed to scare me and talked me out of pursuing acting.

"All along, I secretly waited for my father to come and take me out of my mother's hands."

I was so used to my mother telling me that there was something wrong with me, that I did not even think it affected me. It puzzled me, I laughed it off or did not pay attention to it. It was only during my teenage years that it started to cause me more discomfort. Nevertheless, I thought I still had it better than many other kids. I assumed that most daughters were treated in a similar way by their mothers, and I thought that I somehow deserved what I received. As my mother had said, I was moody and probably exaggerated things. It was my fault that I wasn't the person my mother wanted me to be. I really tried to be the way she would be happy with me, but ultimately, my personality clashed with her values and methods. I was spontaneous, direct, youthfully daring, and ambitious. I liked to express my true feelings and liked to say what I thought. To her, those traits were frightening and foolish. Convinced that human nature was intrinsically evil, in her view never showing one's true colors was a safe policy in any social interaction. I had nothing to hide and being safe was not my priority. From somewhere inside, there lurked a daredevil, eager to explore dangers, remaining philosophical all the while.

I believed in goodness and thought it was perfectly all right to voice my convictions. However, in my mother's view I was required to live and behave according to the victim status that she believed all women had to endure. My idea of my own life was at the other end of the spectrum: it seemed obvious to me that I had an absolute right to be free and entirely myself. In the context of historical and cultural circumstances, my mother was right. Remembrance of the horrors of war, the insidiousness of the Soviet occupation, and the subservient role of a woman in society easily justified my mother's philosophy, which was not at all unique in that time or place. She fitted into society and I did not. I understood where she was coming from, I did not blame her, but had a strong emotional reaction I could not contain. Thinking back on that now, it is easy to see ours as a classic mother-daughter struggle, well placed in the context of those times, but we never talked things over. Discussions quickly turned into arguments, then the arguments slipped into out-of-control, ugly, angry outbreaks on my part.

Fortunately, I was able to keep quite busy and spent a lot of time outside of my home. I usually didn't return until seven or eight in the evening, and went straight to my room to study. I sometimes took a glance at the TV and, at that time of day, there was a program on for young children, hosted by a man who told bedtime stories. One day, I caught myself watching the program for a minute before the story ended and credits showed up. I was mechanically reading the credits when I suddenly saw an unusually familiar name. The actor telling stories was my father! Quite surprised, I exclaimed it loudly to my mother, but she simply shrugged and left the room. I understood she had no intention of having a conversation about it.

Every now and then, I felt a need for my father, so I decided to try to get in touch with him. When I was 16, spontaneously, I went to the phone booth on the street and called the operator to ask for his number. I was too shy to talk to him, but I wanted the number so I could maybe call him later. The operator must have misheard me, because the phone began to ring and my father picked up. When I gave him my name, he said he did not know who I was. Eventually, after several awkward seconds and repeated questions "What? Monika who?", he admitted that he knew who I was, and we engaged in a short conversation. I told him that, within a couple of months, I'd be close to where he lived and I asked if he'd like to get together. I was excited when he agreed, and we set up time and place. He never showed up or called.

The following autumn, my mother announced that my father called her to complain about me having the audacity to contact him. She obviously also disapproved of it and explained to me in her usual superior tone that I would be able to see my father after I completed my university studies. That statement angered me and I rebelled against it childishly: I thought I'd rather skip university altogether, just so she would not think I had succumbed to those ridiculous conditions.

Still, I did not think of myself as an unhappy child or teenager. I did not see my life as bad and I was quickly getting over disappointments. I certainly grew up experiencing frustration and anger in many situations, but usually, when on my own and in a peaceful setting, I had no anger, just a feeling of intense "fire" inside. It was a sense of brightness and power; an overwhelming desire to do what I wanted to do was filling me up. I had relentlessly high energy. My emotions were powerful, but I knew that I also had a strong mind and was feeling confident that I could do whatever I wanted. The urge to get something done felt unstoppable. I was not yet sure what that something would be, but I was burning to make my mark.

Decisions

Decisions about the purpose of my life developed over the years. When I was little, I was sure I'd eventually be united with my parents, enjoy a childhood similar to that of other kids, and then follow in my parents acting footsteps. I knew that I wanted to have children later in life, and would do so after establishing myself in the acting profession. However, as I grew older I noticed that my life simply did not unfold in the way that I had expected. This understanding gave me a more philosophical perspective and a complex view of reality in which desires and needs were not necessarily met, and where awful and very hard-to-explain things like wars and concentration camps were not just nightmares but also a clearly visible and known truth. "What are the limits of human goodness and cruelty? What is my responsibility in life?" There were many more questions, and I wanted to find the answers. From that place of inquiry, I was eventually able to determine the general direction I was heading.

I think I only vaguely understood that most people are looking for happiness. I grew up in a country with a difficult past and present, where endless struggle seemed to be a normal way of life. I did not know exactly what happiness was, and I did not bet on ever finding it. It seemed to be a fleeting, temporary emotion, and I did not associate it with a good career, family, or money but with special, short-lived moments that came unannounced. What I wanted, more than anything else, was the truth, regardless of what that truth was. Thus, it made sense to me to search for that lost point of reference which would explain the cryptic map of life that lay behind me and possibly show options ahead of me for how to proceed.

Since I had no clue what that truth could be, I realized that looking for something so undefined might lead me into all kinds of pitfalls and to erroneous destinations, and maybe even cost me that potential happiness awaiting me if my objectives were already known as achievable. Somehow, the danger did not matter as much as the irresistible prospect of plunging into the unknown in order to learn. Since everybody I knew was busy with more tangible goals, my choice seemed to put me on a solitary path, but I was used to being alone. Inspiration was my trusted companion and guide. I was comfortable with my goal.

"What I wanted, more than anything else, was the truth, regardless of what that truth was."

Soon, I established a belief that practicing art would allow me to work towards discovering the truth I was curious about, and I felt suited to be an artist. Nothing could stop me from painting, but also, in a blatant act of rebellion against my mother, I vowed to pursue many other art forms, including acting.

I was so strongly motivated by my inner drive and sense of purpose that nothing else mattered. Because my mother diligently discouraged me from realizing my dreams, I knew I needed a powerful motivation and I was ready for the hard work ahead. That she pushed on me a vision of a loser was not only incomprehensible but also infuriating. "You are so talented," she said, only to instantly add, with a hint of satisfaction and firmness in her voice, "Too bad nothing will ever come of it." It was hard for me to figure out what she based her opinion on and to believe in what she was saying. I needed to find out who I was by myself and that need taught me a habit of self examination. I carefully observed my reactions and thoughts, analyzed my desires, opinions and decisions. I wanted to make sure that I would always know what I think and feel. To be able to judge myself I compared myself with my friends. When I did that, it looked like I was as capable, both physically and intellectually. My closest friends were also the best students in class, our relationships were good and kind. I cared truly and deeply about people, animals, and all of life. I wanted to put my talents to use for the betterment of the world. All I needed was experience, and I was ready to gain that any way I could. I just could not see anything wrong with all of that.

Still, my mother's words cut deeply and made me feel an internal conflict because I was strongly emotionally connected with her. She was my mother and I naturally desired to trust her and support her in everything she did. All I could do was look forward to the day when I would be on my own, free from her harsh criticisms, and free to prove myself. I could not foresee how extremely difficult it would become.

Artist's License

I was now a young adult eager to dive into the world and realize my potential. I knew already that there was nothing ideal or perfect about this world. It was a chaos full of rules and restrictions, that were imposed either by the iron fist of a political regime, or by a confusing mixture of old and new social standards and codes of behavior. I found the political and social system to be obstructing the progress I needed in order to accomplish my goals. Why couldn't I just do what I wanted to do, without a permission from some authority, that judged me without really knowing me?

"Basically, I made a pact with myself to cultivate my integrity as an artist under any circumstances in order to keep learning and expanding."

One day, in a sudden moment of hilarious reflection on the state of the world, I decided to "issue" myself an artist's license. It was a joke, of course, but it also meant something more to me. I defiantly gave myself the right to explore life as a fully independent artist. So that I could give to the world the pure fruits of my inspiration, I declared myself free to investigate beyond any norms and conventions. Basically, I made a pact with myself to cultivate my integrity as an artist under any circumstances in order to keep learning and expanding. It felt just right that I, obviously, didn't need anybody to give me the artist's license; it was a gift that I gave to myself, with a smirk and a chuckle.

A Library Event

I have experienced several unusual events in my life. I would like to describe a couple of them in this book, as it will help you to better understand what happened to me later, in 1992.

The first event took place in 1973, when I was 16 years old. At this point, I had been painting in oil for a couple of years. I had been studying art history on my own and I was also very interested in the history of philosophy. A great library was within a fifteen-minute walk from my house. There, I browsed through the philosophy books, looking for the oldest recorded accounts I could find. With help of the librarian, I picked two large volumes of Indian Philosophy. In school, we learned about the ancient cultures of Egypt, Greece, and Rome, but I didn't know much about Asian culture, other than in basic outlines.

I examined pages of handwritten text, translations, illustrations, and copies of original Indian materials. The information seemed rather dry and factual with many unknown words and hard to pronounce names. Fortunately, many of the ancient texts were written in verses, in poetic forms of varying lengths, with translations on opposite pages. This drew my attention, and I quickly found myself pulled into the meanings of certain verses. I absorbed them in a flash, with surprising ease. The sentences were about Brahman, the creator, the immovable, yet the mover of all things, and how Atman, the individual soul, connects with Brahman at some point. I read the short description of Atman and Brahman again and then, again, the verses about the unification of the two. In grasping the meaning of the text, I felt a sudden but very smooth surge of uncontainable happiness expanding inside me. Something clicked and a warm, cheerful feeling filled me up. The sense of realization I experienced overwhelmed me. After a short while, the intensity of that cognition grew so much that I could not hold the energy inside any longer. I was completely, helplessly taken over by joy, happiness, and enormous internal power. I could not sit and read anymore, and had to get up. I felt unable to exert any control over myself, which concerned me, as I did not want to start screaming loudly in an, otherwise very quiet library, jump up and down or run around in a frenzy. To avoid all of that, I quickly put the books back on the shelves and ran outside, the energy exploding inside me.

That energy swung me down the library staircase! I hovered above the stairs, feeling no weight under my feet... I had been on the second floor, but it seemed to take only a few seconds to reach the main level. To my astonishment, I had registered every moment of that time, as if it had happened in very slow motion. I fully observed it, but I could not believe it. Flying down, I watched the wall on the right barely moving in front of my eyes, and I saw all the details that I normally did not notice. I was easily examining the nuances of colors and textures, my eyes gazed at tiny bumps on the wall, the stains and scratches moved very slowly in front of me. At the same time, I had to grab the handrail on the left to keep my balance during this rapid, inexplicable flight. The speed of my movement and the detail I could observe seemed impossible to have been able to occur in unison. And yet, it was clearly happening... As it went on, I repeated to myself, "Remember this! Remember this!"

As I opened the door to the street, I found in front of me a very bright, loud, busy world, and I didn't know what to do. Despite my indecision, I noticed that the mighty energy that

I had felt inside kept me lifted and moving somewhere, without my consent. I walked quickly, almost running, the power inside of me pushing me to go fast. I was light as a feather, elated, I looked at my feet and saw them gliding above the pavement; I could not feel the impact of my shoes on the ground.

"The speed of my movement and the detail I could observe seemed impossible to have been able to occur in unison."

A busy intersection, full of traffic, was coming up fast... I had no idea whether my feet would stop, as I had no control over them. All I could do was watch them move, as if of their own volition. That frightened me, because I didn't want to be involved in an accident or cause a collision. I watched myself with fear, but as I quickly neared the curb my feet gently, softly stopped at the edge of the pavement. I still could not feel my weight and still had no idea what would happen next. When the light turned green, I floated across a very busy intersection in the center of a city of almost two million people. I still felt extremely light but I could sense that little by little, my feet had begun to touch the ground. Eventually, by the time I was on the other side of the street, I could feel more of my body weight and walking was slowly getting back to normal.

I accepted that transition with some disenchantment. It was so easy and pleasant to be weightless that the moment of experiencing gravity and its impact was rather uncomfortable.

For the first several seconds I felt heavy and clumsy, but soon I was walking down the street without any strange sensations. Everything was uninterestingly old and "normal" again, but I was still blown away by what had just happened. When I glanced at the window displays in the shops, I felt as if I'd gone on a space trip and then landed back in a familiar place. The experience was sure to never be forgotten but, in the moment, I had no one that I could share it with.

A few weeks later, I had a chance to visit the library again. With anticipation, I opened the same book and looked at the illustrations on the pages close to where I left off. I now know that I was looking at drawings of the subtle body with the chakras but I had no knowledge of that at the time, so I received them as incomprehensible and alien, some even as strange or funny. I could not integrate the knowledge I had about human anatomy with those old Hindu drawings from sometime around 1500 BC, so I just accepted them as something people used to believe in before they learned anatomy, then moved on with my studies without any trace of the sensations that overcame me during my previous visit to the library.

It was important for me to remember that surprising event very clearly, but I did not try to understand it at the time and I left it for later. No one in my life, to my knowledge, had any understanding of such things. Dropped into my "memory box," the event was marked as something very special.

Europe and USA

In 1976, I was supposed to leave Poland to visit London with my boyfriend. Right before we were scheduled to leave, my boyfriend decided not to go. Getting my passport and visa had not been easy, so I got ready to make the trip by myself.

My downstairs neighbor from Warsaw had moved to London, and through her, I was able to rent an inexpensive room to live in. I started to think about staying in London longer than for a month. I arrived there with $400 that my stepfather had given me, and though I wanted to give him the money back quickly, I could not find work that would pay me enough to survive. In Poland, I had worked for my boyfriend's screen printing studio, so I looked for a job in that industry. My first job in London barely paid me enough to cover the expense of getting there by subway and the cost of a meager lunch. It was a grueling, boring job that I utterly hated. I felt lonely in England, but I did not want to go back to Poland, as I could not imagine living with my mother again. It would have been impossible for me to afford living on my own there, and I was happier being in London anyway, even if I was not sure what to do next.

I tried to apply for a job in the fashion design industry, but when I showed my portfolio of fashion drawings, I was told, "We're looking for something... more evolved." My English was not very good, I had no idea what "evolved" meant. Soon, I realized that I had no qualifications to get a job that would secure my survival. I was just a young, inexperienced girl from a disadvantaged Eastern Bloc country; although I knew myself as outspoken I also had a tendency toward introversion and shyness, and my current situation only made me feel more intimidated. I became discouraged and felt lost, but I knew I could not give up. Sometime earlier, I had promised myself to go through anything which would teach me about life and now the opportunity was right in front of me. Despite the trouble I was in, I strongly felt that the whole world was open to me: "All I need to do is find a way to earn a living... and maybe go to art school."

My money was now all gone. I don't know where I'd first heard about topless bars, but I went to visit one in Soho in London. I was quite shocked when they offered me a job on the spot. It consisted of sitting topless and talking to customers while they bought me sugared water, for which they paid top dollar. It seemed so odd. Yes, I was naïve, but hungry to learn. I wanted to become tough, smart, and experienced. My artist's license became very handy: I felt I broke some kind of enormous taboo and opened the door to the forbidden world, that I knew that none of my high school friends would consider entering.

"Sometime earlier, I had promised myself to go through anything which would teach me about life and now the opportunity was right in front of me."

Although somewhat embarrassed about my new job, I managed to save enough money to enroll in art school. Just around that time, my Polish boyfriend visited me. He was nine years older than I was, and since meeting him, a couple of years prior, he had become a father figure and mentor to me. Being in love with him gave me a release from the depressing influence of my mother and the emotional support that I received from him gave me confidence. I had missed him a lot, and while I did not intend to, I became pregnant during his visit. He did not want to get married, and I was emotionally unable to go through with an abortion. "No matter what happens", I told myself, "I am going to have this baby, just because it feels like the right thing to do".

My mother was furious at me over my decision. She wrote me a couple letters about how stupid I was, how I didn't know what I was doing, and exclaimed that I was driving her to tear her hair out in despair. Her messages affected me terribly, but because of the precious life inside of me, I was able to calm myself down.

My boyfriend had to return to Poland but I wanted to stay in London and wait for him to come back. He did not get the visa and I eventually managed to go back to Warsaw just days before my due date. My daughter was born there. Little by little I found that I did not fit well into the role of a housewife. I constantly felt inspired to paint, to learn, and to discover myself through art. I did not detest cooking and cleaning like my mother did, but it did not come naturally to me. Once again,

I was not the person that I had been expected to be, this time for my boyfriend. I loved him and wanted to spend the rest of my life taking care of my little family, but something wasn't working.

We engaged in many arguments, and he began to pull away. I was told that if I wanted to be an artist I should not have a family. He had relatives in the United States and went there for vacation, leaving me with our daughter in his Warsaw apartment. I was able to get in touch with him only several months later.

The political and economic situation in Poland was complicated and the future of the country uncertain. Many people were leaving, in search for better lives. My passport was only valid for a few more days, so my daughter and I left Poland and moved to Amsterdam. Upon arrival, a friend by association was able to accommodate us in his home, and he helped me a lot with the transition.

Life with my daughter felt good and natural. We shared a beautiful, harmonious closeness, a strong and loving bond. She was a calm, sweet child, independent like me, and a quick learner. Because I greatly valued the asset of self-sufficiency, I wanted to instill in her the capacity to fulfill her own desires as much as possible, without waiting for help from me or anyone else. She was not yet two years old when I saw her try to reach the light switch before walking into a dark room. She knew I was nearby and watching, but instead of waiting for me to turn the light on, she acted on her own by finding a long stick in the kitchen and using that to reach the switch.

When my boyfriend returned to Poland half a year later, I wanted to leave Holland so that we could be together again, but he no longer wanted it. When I asked if he missed me and our daughter, he said he did not have such feelings. Then he stated that our relationship was over. My world shattered. After that conversation, the only thing I could focus on was making sure my daughter had the chance to develop a bond with her father. I had not grown up with such a bond and I strongly felt I needed to prevent my daughter from experiencing the same. I held on to what he had promised back in England, that he wanted to raise our child, and I took my daughter back to Poland for two months, so she could be with her daddy. Separating with her was extremely hard. I could not forget the look she gave me at the moment of my departure. I could tell she was scared because I was leaving, but she did not cry. I reassured her, told her that she would be fine and that I would be back soon, and I knew she understood. "It is only for two months, just two months, I kept on telling myself".

Within a month of our separation, a military coup broke out in Poland. The Solidarity Movement led an uprising against the government, the borders were suddenly closed and communication cut off, rendering it impossible to get in touch with people inside the country. I knew if I went back there at that time, I would have not been able to leave again. There was no telling what the results of the uprising would be. People spoke of a possibility of Russian invasion, of an already bad situation getting worse. Though I wanted to be with my daughter, I had to wait.

It took a year for Poland to stabilize and for the borders to open. During this time, I had assumed that my daughter was living with her father, but one day I learned with a surprise, that she was with my mother and stepfather. I had mixed feelings about it and I was not sure what to do. My mother was retired and received plenty of support from her husband. They lived quiet lives and had a summer house in the countryside. They were entirely capable of providing for a child, and I knew my mother took very good care of her and that my daughter probably still spent a lot of time with her father as well. When I spoke to my mother on the phone, she sounded happy. In the end I assumed that my mother wanted to help me. I knew that she was not happy with me when I was a child, but she seemed to be pleased with her granddaughter. "She told me she loves me," my mother said, sounding surprised and amused. I had told my daughter that every night, and she'd learned it well. It seemed my family in Poland was fine. My daughter was surrounded by people with organized, settled lives, and she was receiving good care.

I was nervous, heartbroken, and needed to make money right away, so that I could create a stable and healthy environment in which to raise my child. On the other hand, I also needed to keep painting. Working on and off in the nightclub again came to my rescue. I was in a constant emotional discomfort, but dancing on stage, entertaining customers and making money allowed me to look forward to better times. A girlfriend of mine who lived in Paris offered to let me share her apartment for a year. It gave me a chance to prepare for and pass the exam to the Academie des Beaux Artes in Paris. Soon after, I met a group of talented young painters from Germany, traveled with them to Cologne, and started painting under the influence of a strong wave of postmodernism. I was immediately taken by the explosive energy of the art scene in Cologne. It felt like I was in the right place at the right time. I was learning fast and my identity as an artist was quickly starting to take shape; I did not go back to Paris. Together with a few young Dutch artists, I shared studios in Amsterdam, and I soon had my own one-person show in a well-known gallery in the center of the city. I worked very hard and exhausted myself, but it was precisely what I needed to do. I often struggled to make the ends meet but kept on hoping for some kind of breakthrough so I could have my daughter with me.

Times were changing quickly and my art was going through a fast metamorphosis as well. I eventually tired of the impersonal social commentary that was often the main theme of the postmodern era, and realized I needed to search deeper into myself and find support in my inner being. I had never done that before, but with the new skills of the neo-expressionist style, I became successful with a series of abstract paintings which I titled "Deep Paintings." The Royal Dutch Collection in Den Haag purchased one of my pieces and I began to feel that my existence was justified, at least socially, and I gained confidence that I was on the right track with my work.

The situation was far from perfect, but I felt stronger and decided to go back to Poland and bring my daughter back with me. I knew she was used to living with my mother and stepfather, but I thought our relationship was so close that she would certainly want to be with me. As I saw it, we belonged together. I envisioned that it would be the same as what I had experienced when I was living with my grandma and the time came to move in with my mom. My grandmother helped me make the transition, and I expected my mother to do the same.

I called my mother to let her know I was coming to visit and get my daughter but, to my surprise, she advised me not to come. She quickly explained that my ex-boyfriend's wife was going to be jealous. What? I was used to my mother saying strange, hurtful things that made no sense but, how could I even consider not going back to where I was from and where my family was for that kind of reason? When I got to Poland, I was shocked to realize that my daughter did not want to leave with me. Only then did I understand what had really happened, and it confused me greatly. "Why did you take her away from me?" I asked my mother, unable to disguise my despair. "You can be with her when I die," she stated permissibly. As eerie as that statement was, in my mother's rendition it sounded like a common-sense pronouncement and just another reminder of how clueless I was. My child had been conditioned not to go with me, and even though she was only 6 years old, I felt she deserved the freedom of choice. All that time, my mother had been creating an emotional connection with my daughter that did not include me, and now she was unwilling to let my daughter live with me. I realized that things were set up according to her plan, and I could not bear to take my daughter with me against her own will.

This short conversation, regarding the custody of my daughter, took place in the country house. When it was over I ran out into the woods. Out there, no one could hear me screaming at the top of my lungs. The emotional complexity of the situation was clear to me, but the pain was unbearable.

My flight back to Amsterdam was a few days later. I spent the rest of my stay in Poland crying. It annoyed my mother, and as I departed, she told me she was happy to be rid of me.

"Shocked and shattered but unable to change the situation, I plunged into my art and let it guide me."

The truth is, when I was younger, I was willing to go through any difficulty just to learn, feel, and gain experience. I was almost eager to suffer just to discover what suffering was. I was ready to love to find out what love was, and I was ready to lose love just to find out how it felt. In a childish way, I needed to know all that, so I could grow up. Losing the love of my life, which was how I thought of my daughter's father, and being separated from my dearest child was hard to bear, for years to come. Shocked and shattered but unable to change the situation, I plunged into my art and let it guide me. The urge to overcome the devastation I felt was supported by constant inspiration. I painted to get through each day. I held onto the belief that working on my paintings would eventually pay off and allow me to be with my daughter.

In 1984, I met David, who became my boyfriend and best friend. There was a new dawn, a new hope, and new place to live. In 1986, we moved to United States, where David was from. We were a lot alike, and our similarities deepened our relationship and drew us very close, but because the similarities included being stubborn and hotheaded, we would often fight. Eventually, we could not agree on the next move and simply went our separate ways, so we could each do what we felt was best for ourselves. David went to New York City, where he planned to get involved in film production, and I took a Greyhound to Los Angeles. We kept in touch, and I thought we would get back together at some point, but it never happened.

When I arrived in L.A., a new chapter of my life began. I did not know what I was going to do. I considered pursuing acting and modeling, and even caught the interest of a known modeling agency, but acting was more interesting to me so I started to go to auditions. It didn't take me long to realize that looking for an acting job meant dealing with obnoxious producers, even if they were representing legitimate productions. Several times, I found myself a subject of a hidden agenda, indirectly pressured to offer sexual favors in exchange for a possible chance at a role. Once, during an audition, the casting director excused himself and left the room. When he returned a few minutes later, he was naked. Needless to say, that was not in the script I was given, and as hilarious as it may seem now, the whole scene disgusted me at the time. The topless bar in London, from years before, seemed more benign and ethical in comparison. I decided to take it easy with auditions for the time being. I got a job in a print shop and started to think about painting again. Soon, I was able to rent a cheap, never-before-inhabited attic in an old Victorian mansion to live in and use as a studio.

Abstract Dimension

Since the event that took place in the library in Poland, I had experienced similar occurrences that were both revelatory and hard to explain. Sometimes in my dreams, I gained historical information I'd never read about before. Once, for example, I dreamt about ancient China and its sacred rituals and customs, something I knew nothing about. The information I later read on the subject was identical, only less detailed than what I saw in my dream. What I learned in my dreams included words in Chinese I had never known before, and these words turned out to be correct and had been used in the proper context. Though events of this kind had made various levels of impact on my life, what occurred one day in 1988 was much more significant.

Since my arrival in L.A., I had come up with over thirty titles of potential poems that would reflect my impressions of Los Angeles, as well as other subjects of contemplation. Once I had a space to paint, I settled into a new painting routine, and those poem titles became the inspiration for a series of small acrylics. I liked the process of looking through several different titles and finding one I wanted to illustrate with paint on a canvas rather than words on a page. Some of the new paintings resembled surrealism, but they also maintained the postmodernist tradition of a rather critical examination of society and culture.

I had six or seven paintings done when I picked a new title, "Understanding Understatement". I liked its playfulness and the challenge it presented, though it was hard to imagine what it might look like. I began by trying to envision the meaning of "understanding". I made a straight line, initially to symbolize one decisive thought, then added other straight lines that crossed each other at various angles. That group of lines (thoughtful decisions) became a basic image of an "understanding". I extended colored shading from each, transparent enough so many lines and shades were still visible in varying degrees. The shading could have different meanings, but at that point, to me, it embodied the perceived emotional content of the thoughts. Those premises were not final conclusions in any way; they simply allowed me to get into the painting and see where it led me. In this manner, the general sketch of the painting appeared on canvas.

I was deeply into creating the painting, watching it grow as I was still adding more lines and shades, when something most extraordinary took place. While maintaining complete awareness, I watched the painting become something else. Suddenly, it escaped the full, attentive scope of my vision and expanded beyond the title and its meaning. What I was looking at in no time outgrew me and all my knowledge. The image was there just as I painted it, and I was looking at it, but the insight I suddenly possessed was not coming from my own understanding. It was there for me to see, but it was not mine.

As I was working on "Understanding Understatement", something sprang up from outside of my vision. It superimposed itself, aligned, and completely took over the image I had created. After a moment of careful observation, I came to understand that what I was looking at now was the totality of all existing phenomena in a form of abstract imagery. I witnessed the abstract forms alive, being created continually, eternally existing in their own dimension of extraordinary, illuminating energy. I grasped their sense by using an intuitive code that somehow became clear to me in an instant.

**"The profound, expansive, and enlightening dimension
I visited through the painting was beyond anything
that I had ever previously thought possible."**

I realized that under some circumstances, the mind can enter an abstract dimension of perception, a field of strictly intellectual content. It is a sphere of consciousness in which all things have their conceptual beginnings. In that space, our minds unite with a universal essence that exists on a certain vibrational level. That essence is pure brilliance, as it perceives all events and spontaneously creates new ones as well. It is an ever-active sphere of creation, with thoughts as its vehicle. The profound, expansive, and enlightening world I visited through the painting was beyond anything that I had ever previously thought possible.

Throughout many years of working on paintings and staring at them, I have made many discoveries and have had revelations of all kinds. Often, I was also feeling desperate and lost, unable to make any progress, but still painting away, even when feeling really dumb about it. Now, however, all my perseverance, all my previous attempts and successes, seemed significant only as means to that singular discovery. It appeared that I somehow tapped into the creative force behind all that exists. From my experience of viewing art, old or new, I knew that specific energy can be felt in great works. No one part of a masterpiece is the "great" part; rather, the whole entity exudes the magical force of creation. My own experience making art was not about creating something great, (that would have been a rather pretentious aspiration) but about learning and reaching new levels of discovery, if possible, a painting at a time. Now, it was about breaking through to the normally invisible spectrum and grasping it.

By the time this happened, I had studied modernism and abstract art and knew it possibly dealt with other dimensions of perception, but I had had no idea it was something that exists as an energy field one can tap into, just as I did that day. I didn't interpret my experience as spiritual, but I eventually realized that abstract art, which was discovered at the very end of the nineteenth century and took the world by storm during the first fifty years of the twentieth, started out as mystical and spiritual insight. The Swedish artist and mystic Hilma af Klimt considered her abstract compositions as tools of communication with beings from another dimension. Kasimir Malevich, a Polish/Russian artist, left behind any trace of figuration in art for the sake of simplest geometrical forms, meant to embody "pure feeling" and eventually, in his futuristic vision, replace the need for God. Dutch painter Piet Mondrian achieved pure abstraction while being very involved in Christian theosophy and the spiritual teachings of Madame Blavatsky. Modernism was born out of a discovery of another plane of perception. Over the course of the twentieth century, many artists were influenced by Asian culture and its spiritual traditions and their work was also a pure abstraction.

I had no mentors or teachers, nor did I look for inspiration in Asian tradition. I cannot claim modernists in general or any particular artists as my influences. Still, to my own surprise, the little painting that started the series of non-objective works in 1988 looked like some kind of cubist composition and even resembled Malevich's constructivist works. Sometime later, I learned that a Merkabah, the tetrahedron star made up of two tetrahedrons, supposedly led to perception of other dimensions. I guess it worked in my case, but I had no idea that what I was looking at could even be a tetrahedron; it was neither intentional nor really a true tetrahedron or a Merkabah. Maybe the angles of some of the crossing lines and my shading evoked the realization of abstract dimension...

Regardless of those associations, the actual effect I experienced was a huge breakthrough in the development of my artwork, my method of creating, and my understanding of my art-making. The experience took my work to a new level, and whatever happened before was just the path that led me to that moment.

After my discovery of abstract dimension, everything else, including acting and modeling prospects, seemed trivial. The depth and illuminating power I experienced, the aliveness of it and the sense of exhilarating expansion and profound joy that accompanied it, were worth all my devotion and wakeful service. I dedicated the next four years strictly to the relentless process of visual exploration that started that day with "Understanding Understatement."

1988 to 1992

My experience in 1992 was spontaneous, but that does not mean that nothing facilitated it. It was spontaneous in the sense that I did not intentionally make it happen. I had no idea something like that could even happen. The events and situations that eventually led to it are worth noting, even if my personal story is not of a great importance compared to the result. Some circumstances and their succession are good to take notice of, as they made me intuitively engage in practices which later proved essential in the process of self-realization.

Slowly, I was gaining my bearings in the L.A. art scene. A gallery/interior design store in West Hollywood asked me to put figures or objects in my abstract work because that way my paintings would be more attractive to buyers and the store was interested in showing them. I took the challenge and the result was good. From then on, my work was divided into semi-figurative art which I was lucky to sell from time to time, and abstract art purely for art's sake. I hoped that the latter would eventually be recognized for what it was.

Later in 1990, I quit my job. The art print company did not fare well in the economic hit of the stock market crashes, and art sales had dropped. Work was slow, and I no longer felt needed there. I also wanted to spend more time on my paintings. Soon, I fell into a decent rhythm of living and breathing my artwork. Sometime at the beginning of 1991, I sold four of my non-objective pieces to a collector and New York City gallery owner at an art fair in the L.A. Convention Center. I had to set my prices quite low, but it felt like a good start. Other than that, I was now 34 years old, living on a shoestring budget in a city in which I did not know many people, spending most of the time by myself. Events like sales or shows were sporadic.

Those years in L.A. were the loneliest years of my life. Instinctively, I knew I was in the right state of being to give proper attention to my artwork, but a very important part of my private life often made the solitude feel heavy, with lingering pain and a growing sense of guilt. My beloved daughter was still living in Poland with my mother, and she was growing up without me. My relationship with my mother had not improved and contacting her usually left me feeling depressed for weeks at the time. I kept in touch as much as I could through phone calls, letters, and packages. I often felt like part of me was numb. It had to be that way, so I could go on. Other times pain and anger would fill me up, wear me out, and leave me depressed.

I wanted to be financially stable enough to be able to be with my daughter and repay my mother for taking care of her for so long, but since I was barely surviving on my own this was not an easy goal to accomplish. When I was leaving Poland, I gave myself a deadline of thirteen years, thinking that would be a perfectly sufficient amount of time, to establish myself fully as a successful artist and to help my family financially. After about twelve years of working very hard, having sacrificed comforts or sense of security, I was living in an attic without a kitchen, bathroom, or running water and I was broke, with no foreseeable changes ahead. I knew I was accomplishing something important (at least to me) in my art but, I was barely managing to stay alive. I lived on limited rations of oatmeal and canned tuna fish and did little other than paint in my studio, stare at the painting on the easel, and then, stare at it again. Even when my work was going well and I was pleased with my progress, depression would creep up on me anyway. Still, I persisted, painting every day, regardless of how I felt.

"Instinctively, I knew I was in the right state of being to give proper attention to my artwork, but a very important part of my private life often made the solitude feel heavy, with lingering pain and a growing sense of guilt."

The discipline I had self-imposed was bringing interesting results. While painting, I was sometimes able to re-enter the place where I could sense and perceive that exhilarating, phenomenal sphere of abstract thought. It would usually start with a sudden appearance of an image from somewhere in my past, a location I had once been in, along with some connected emotions. I'd recognize the setting with a surprise and instantly felt the emotion I had experienced when being in that place. When that happened, I felt the energy flowing through my brush and being released into the painting. At those moments time seemed to stop. While looking at the place on the painting where the emotion went in, I could feel again the brilliance of that nonobjective, live dimension, and, at times, I could even dwell in that space. My work became my life, my paintings were the ground on which I stood. The truth I spent so many years searching for had, in part, become my reality. I was in awe living it because I had never been able to even imagine such a possibility before. Every time I worked on a painting, I knew there was chance that an independent entity could come into being. I also knew that the energy and consciousness of that entity was not coming from me exactly; I was just aware enough to let it go through me into the painting. I was participating in a creative act which was beyond my full comprehension, but I was the one to get its radiant and exhilarating message. So much phenomenal information was being transmitted! It was information coded visually, to be grasped through the process of "visual thinking". The learning was infinite, and filled me with clarity, lightness, and power. The next step was to share it. I was hoping people who looked at those paintings would also get the message.

The little circle of people I knew in the "art world" seemed to have positive opinions about my work, but it was not helping me to generate any sales. My attempts to find a gallery that would represent me were unsuccessful. One of my paintings was published in a known art magazine but no interest followed. I was expecting to participate in a group show sometime at the beginning of 1992 and was hoping for that event to bring me some success. I was living off the sales of my half-figurative works sold to anybody I could, and for any price I could get. Sales were completely unpredictable. I never knew if I was going to be able to pay the rent, eat, or be able to buy art supplies. In my studio, I was often depressed, not knowing what else to do to improve my finances, to survive, to be with my daughter, or to help my mother; even though my mother and stepfather were retired and living comfortably, I felt guilty for not contributing more financially.

During the second half of 1991, I began to sink into despair for more substantial periods of time. I was living an artist's life and that felt natural but motherhood had also been something that felt natural and not being a present parent for my daughter felt like a terrible loss for both of us. Although I was not with her in person, I somehow felt like I was always with her regardless how far away she was. My heart never left her and the connection was always there. I was unhappy to be without her but at the same time I was very happy she existed, wherever she was. In my heart, I always carried a strong, positive image of my child, I trusted her and always envisioned the best for her.

For years I thought that the problem I had with my mother was exclusively a matter of our incompatibility and that I was an unruly child, a person difficult to get along with. I assumed my mother's relationship with my daughter was different, because my daughter was naturally more peaceful, agreeable and easy. In time, though, I began to worry that I was letting my daughter experience the same negativity that I'd experienced as a child. In the past, I did not call it negativity, but simply a pessimistic view, which my mother defended as a wiser way of living. Eventually, I began to realize my mother's pessimism might not have been as healthy as she insisted it was. Knowing that my child was subjected to it without me being able to improve the situation, was hard to bear.

Throughout my childhood and youth my sense of spirituality was very unclear. Living in a Catholic country like Poland, however, one is naturally exposed to the figure and myth of Jesus Christ, regardless of one's own religious attitude. It was this way even when the communist regime actively prohibited religion. I instinctively agreed with Jesus's teachings but was not sure of their practicality. I knew how to say a prayer because my grandmother taught me once, and I remembered it. I liked the prayer but saw my mother rolling her eyes when grandma taught me, so to be in line with my mother's preferences, I never prayed.

As I mentioned earlier, what I was learning in school about history and politics was contradicting the information I was getting from home. It is probably because of all of those conflicting theories and views, that I did not believe anything written or said without questioning it. My top priority was to keep my mind independent. I did not want to get indoctrinated by any society into any particular belief. As an adult, living in different countries and traveling a lot helped me to maintain an outsider's view. My ideal approach was empirical study. I tried not to make any conclusions before I had an experience which would give me certainty.

I was curious about invisible aspects of life but neither in a religious or atheist way. I was careful and did not want to believe in anything, but I didn't want to exclude anything as a possibility either. Shortly before leaving Poland as a teenager, I found myself relating well to basic Buddhist principles. The ethics of Buddhist behavior attracted me in the same way Jesus's teachings did, but from what I then understood,

Buddhism was too passive as a way of being for me. I had a natural predisposition towards physical activity and was rather restless. The only way I would accept sitting in one spot for a long time was while staring at a painting in progress, still getting up on occasion to change something, add a stroke, a layer, something, then sit and stare at it again...

I did not believe in powers other than dedication and hard work, which I thought, when applied, should yield tangible results. I had ambitions and plans I wanted to realize and my focus was on the ways to achieve my goals, which by then were quite practical. I wanted to do a good job and be rewarded for it materially, well enough to be able to be with my child, maintain my art studio and keep on growing as an artist.

In some way, I believed we were possibly spirits but having no proof of it, I treated those beliefs as my mystical, visionary fantasies based on strong intuitive impulses and used them in some of my writings. I even wrote two movie scripts based on the premises of the reincarnation of an individual spirit and on psychic powers. Still, nothing was certain as far as my understanding of spirituality. I felt a sense of wonder and surprise at the glimpses of those unexplainable sensations. There was an underlying notion that something else could be going on beyond the visible and solid reality. The unusual dreams and psychic experiences I had were all very interesting. Sometimes, I was startled by a vivid dream that I could interpret symbolically or shocked by the accuracy of my psychic predictions. I was also often afraid of them because I did not know why and how they came to me. I could not control them. In the same way, my intuitive choices came from a place I could not argue with rationally but had to simply follow as directed. If they got me in trouble, I just blamed myself for being stupid. I did not see them as legitimate spiritual guidance.

"There was an underlying notion that something else could be going on beyond the visible and solid reality. "

Overall, I lived a very secular existence, with painting being possibly the closest thing to spiritual practice, even though I wouldn't describe it that way. If I claimed painting was my religion, it only meant I was serious about it and worked on it all the time.

In L.A. I had a small group of friends, who were mostly artists. I met people all the time, but I was very focused on my work and that's what I spent my time doing. I did not have any lasting intimate relationships and, looking back, I don't think I was interested in a serious relationship right then. My occupation and family became my priorities, and a love relationship was a distant dream. I poured all my energy into my artwork and diligently worked toward some kind of resolution that would change my life for the better. I knew what I was doing artistically, but my struggle to survive and accomplish my goals was very consuming and frustrating. With my unusual family situation and my recent artistic discoveries and developments, I could not compare it to anyone else's life. I felt lonely in the fight for survival, and there seemed to be

CHAPTER I: MY LIFE BEFORE THE EXPERIENCE

no progress. I retreated into my isolation without any feasible solutions in sight. I often felt down, heavy, and so sluggish that I did not even want to get out of bed. That depressing state kept going for months and was getting worse. I needed to change something to get better.

At the end of 1991, I designed a diet for myself that I hoped would revitalize me. Throughout the months of January and February of 1992, for two days in a row, I consumed only liquids: water, liquid soup, milk, juices, weak tea and coffee, smoothies, etc. On the third day, I ate whatever I wanted, without any restrictions. The next day, I would repeat the process. Overall, I think it did indeed revive me and made me feel stronger. I liked it. The diet was tough to follow, but applying the discipline was helpful. It kept me in better emotional control. I also lost weight and felt lighter and more agile.

On March 1st, the group art show that I was participating in, ended. I did not sell anything. It was a show in a good gallery and I had high hopes connected to it. The hopes vanished and helplessness replaced them. I dropped into a state of deep depression. I was breaking down.

PART TWO:

The Experience

CHAPTER II: KUNDALINI PROCESS

The Day of March 10th

**'I said to myself, "No matter what happens,
I am going to watch this".'**

I woke up sensing the nervous breakdown closer than ever before. I could not find peace. I knew that thirteen years had gone by and I had not realized my goals. I had failed. Nothing else mattered. All my years of incredible personal sacrifices, striving to break through my misfortunes and hardships just to have a better life - to be with my child, to have basic comforts to continue working, to be recognized for my efforts and achievements, to feel like I belonged somewhere - had not helped. Although I did experience a breakthrough in my work and had reached a place I never even knew existed, that realization left me feeling even lonelier, because I was not able to bring my work to the platform from which it could have its raison d'être in society. I did not feel anyone cared about the results of my efforts and I began to think that I had no reason to exist either. My survival was bleak and painful and I could not see my future in a good light. I was on a path to total demise.

I started to have suicidal thoughts. At first, they would come and go, but eventually they settled in and there was nothing but suicidal thoughts and strong inclinations to do something to fulfill the urge. I hated myself and blamed myself for failing. Eventually, the thoughts of killing myself became the only thoughts that made sense to me. At the same time, the idea horrified me. I had always been a positive person who considered suicide an unacceptable escape. Now, as I found myself in an emotional state of overwhelming discomfort, it felt like the only way of coping was to end the torture. Being someone who acts once decision is made, I was ready to proceed. Yet, another part of me was still fighting what I had come to think of as an inevitable turn of events. I spent the whole morning and early afternoon of that day trying to stop myself from figuring out the best way to end my life. Still, at around 2:20 pm I was ready to get razor blades. I did not have any in my place. In an effort to resist that plan, or at least delay it, and not go to the store right away, I decided to take a shower. I was not at all in a mood for it, but taking a shower was always a good cure for agitation. Contact with water had been soothing to me. I needed to do whatever I could to stop myself from what I thought was the only right thing to do.

The house was empty, as usual. I walked downstairs to the bathroom. It contained an old, ceramic tub with tall, translucent glass walls around it. There was a nicely sized window that was partly covered in vines. The light seeping through lit the room sufficiently, but the shadow cast by the greenery made it dimmer.

As I was taking off my clothes, I saw a large cockroach slowly, arduously climbing the wall behind the tub. It was not the first time I'd seen one in the bathroom, as it was nothing unusual in L.A.. I knew it was not going to get closer or fall into the tub, but seeing it solidified my mood. My reality was that I was watching a huge cockroach climbing the wall and I felt repulsed by it, but I felt even more repulsed by myself. I slowly, silently climbed into the tub, absently turned on the water without plugging the drain, and just lay down, collapsing in resignation. All along, all I could do was try to comply with the order I had given myself on the way to the bathroom: I would not allow negative emotion to take over my mind. I had to make a very conscious effort to push away the suicidal thoughts, which was very difficult. It was like working on a painting but feeling completely lost and seeing no progress. I knew instinctively that I had to keep trying. I had trained my mind to paint in any emotional state. Throughout the years, I often felt very sad or frustrated but could work anyway. I had learned how to work through it. This time, I had to use the techniques I already knew to help me hold off bad feelings. It worked for only a few seconds at a time. When I noticed I was again slumping into violent despair, unable to stand the pressure inside me, I tried to abandon that state by moving away from it. I noticed that what I moved into instead was a state of nothingness, a neutral space, neither good nor bad. That was the best I could do. I had no positive feelings inside and could not even imagine anything good. To evoke a neutral stance for mere seconds at a time took all of my effort. I tried to have my mind guard that desolate, empty space from another wave of agony.

I had to monitor myself carefully in order to cope with my unbearable condition. I had to acknowledge my emotional state, then work to move away from it enough to be able to maintain my sanity. I recognized it for what I thought it was: depression. That label was enough to pinpoint it and let me feel its power, to hold it by its name and to know its nature. When I managed to keep that emotion away for a moment, an empty state of no emotions was invariably the result.

When I noticed myself tending to my emotional state by refusing to dwell on it, the thoughts still ran rampant through my mind. I knew what they were saying and where they were leading me, urging me to get out of the tub right then and run to the store for razor blades. They were scolding me for procrastinating. All I could do was move away from the macabre feeling that caused the thoughts to grow and multiply. Once that took place, I was left just breathing. Shortly, the obviousness of my fate showed itself clearly again...

After lying in the tub for about ten minutes, I felt I was losing the fight. I could not pretend anymore. I did not want to live, but there I was. Like a useless object with a negative value, I existed despite myself. Death seemed better than my life, and I was ready to proceed, but then, out of the blue, I came up with something that I thought might help: to try to release the impossible-to-handle energy inside me with an orgasm. Depressed for months and devoid of any sexual desire, I thought this new idea was absurd. I was apprehensive, but it appeared as if some kind of inner order forced me to act, so I tried. Nothing happened. "Even that didn't work" was my thought. I just lay numb, my eyes closed, my life forlorn.

From time to time, I again tried to figure out what I'd done wrong to end up this way. I deeply regretted that I was unable to go back in time and fix any mistakes I'd made. The waves of remorse, shame, and guilt resurfaced, making me squirm. I was still able to push the negative emotion away, but I could not escape my thoughts. In a maniacal mode, memories of important decisions, deeds, situations, and relationships came in flashbacks. I attempted to examine them, to try to figure out again and again what I'd done wrong, but I received no results. I kept lying there, "spat out", accepting the torture with resignation. Seconds and minutes were like an eternity spent in awareness of the truth and the pain that it brought.

Eventually, I had to fully admit to myself that death was there, ready for me. It was pointless to reach for something I did not believe in anymore - my life. I was not who I always thought I was - an artist on the way to success. I was a total loser, unable to have a family, unable to support myself and my child, unable to keep on living.

I had come to the end of the road and had no choice but to give in. I had nothing to look forward to and I could not turn back. The energy inside of me was uncontrollable, and I had no access to it, no understanding of it. If minutes before there still was a stubborn desire to live left within me, making me try once more to fight with my self-imposed death sentence, it was now crushed. I had lost. My fight was over, and I had to accept my death. There was no choice.

There I was, in the bathroom of a house where the other tenants barely knew me. I was just one person in a city of over twelve million, someone overcome by a sense of complete and utter loss. Time ticked by silently as I continued to lay in the tub. Eventually, condemned to the inevitable next step, I opened my eyes, lifted my head, and blankly stared in front of me. Right there, I instantly saw something shocking, something that made me freeze in terror.

In the silence and confinement of the old, bare bathroom, my eyes got fixed on the white wall of the tub. On that background, a rope of lambent rainbow light was moving slowly. It was somewhere between one and two inches in diameter and moved with a constant speed. As I kept on staring, I noticed it seemed to originate in my crotch and loop around my legs, twisting and turning quite beautifully. At times, it reached above the edge of the tub, then spread around my body in wider loops.

I continued examining it, with detached and clinical judgment. The terrifying part was that I could very clearly tell that what I was looking at was not of the world I knew; it was outside my habitual scope of influence and awareness. It came from some world I had no knowledge of. It was completely beyond my experience and understanding, beyond everything I knew. Even the event four years prior, my breakthrough while painting, was more understandable, mind blowing as it was. That experience offered a vision that came from my own painting. It seemed to be naturally related to my focus on the creative process, so I could accept it. It was unexpected and unbelievable, but still a natural development of my visual quest.

"The terrifying part was that I could very clearly tell that what I was looking at was not of the world I knew; it was outside my habitual scope of influence and awareness. "

This time, while I was in a state of full agreement with my impending death and in complete surrender to it, there were no rainbows anywhere close to my imagination. I could not trace any connection between my state of being and the beautiful, serpentine ray of light glowing and dancing peacefully. My reality was not even bleak anymore. It was senseless, hollow, and doomed. Nevertheless, I found myself surrounded by a dense flow of rainbow light, clearly visible and gliding gently. Anyone who has ever been faced with a completely startling, surreal occurrence might be able to relate to what I felt. The fear paralyzed me, and I could only watch in shock. The light was not bright or blinding, but was still clear and defined. As it swirled slowly around me, my obvious and instant reaction was to run away as quickly as possible. I jumped up in horror before I knew I was doing it. Terrified, I immediately turned off the running water and reached for the sliding door. I was getting out of the tub as quickly as I could, but when the door was half-open and I was taking a step out, I noticed, with complete disbelief, that the rainbow was moving with me! Just as I initially thought, the light was coming out of me, flowing and moving above me, clinging to my body at times and then flowing gently away from it. I saw it circulating through me and realized that I could not possibly separate myself from it. It was part of me! Seeing that made me think of two options: I could freak out and release the terror I felt by jumping out of the bathroom and into the empty hall, screaming as loudly as possible, or I could... conquer my fear. After a moment I made the decision to stay in place. I said to myself, "No matter what happens, I am going to watch this". I closed the sliding door and sat down in the tub again. This time I crossed my legs and faced the wall with the window.

I was ready to accept whatever followed, and my full attention held me motionless. My eyes were open, and I looked ahead of me, waiting to see what might happen. Seconds went by, and I calmed down, unsure if anything else would take place. Suddenly, my vision began to fill with pictures, images in motion, like a movie. I saw a small child, then heard that child's thoughts in my head. I watched the child from behind, I saw him/her react to something. As the imagery continued, I began to recognize the situations that the child encountered. I realized, with great surprise, that the child was me.

In that moment, I saw myself like I had never seen myself before, from a distance. I was able to watch myself and relive moments from my past, in chronological order, recovered in full in my memory. I saw my father in the time he visited when I was a little over 2 years old. He had asked me to come with him, which upset me greatly because I knew that I couldn't. I cried so hard that day. My mother tried to distract me by taking pictures of me. Next, I recalled the incident with our dog and the leash, when I made the decision to never hurt anything again. I witnessed events from my elementary school and my high school years, when I made decisions and placed questions in my "memory box," waiting for a chance to analyze them when I felt more in power. The episodes appeared one after the other. Each scene had to do with a specific thought that had a consequence, that had created a need for me to make an important decision about some aspect of my life. Some of the images I remembered well; they had been in my thoughts as I was growing up. Others, I recognized only as they appeared to me as if some other source of information supplied my memory and made me watch my life over again.

"The process took place of its own volition, and I just attended it with my mind, much to my own astonishment."

Within a few minutes, I'd scrolled through my whole life, thought after thought. I had no problem viewing each event and reliving them as if they were happening in that present moment. The events, thoughts, and decisions were harmoniously connected; I saw them clearly and comprehended my choices that resulted from the consequential order. I realized that, in the course of my life, my decisions were not mistakes; rather, they were exactly what I should have done, and my reactions to the situations and judgments were accurate. Now, as I thoroughly observed each again, I knew they were all right, that my thinking was ethical and justified, even if I had ended up hurting myself as a result. The times I reacted in anger or despair were clearly justified as well. I knew all along that my decisions often went beyond logical deduction. They were not always rational, and the conclusions were not results of any generalized truths or customarily learned mental procedures. However, they addressed each situation in the way that was the best for everything and everyone and left my path free from unnecessary entanglements. I noticed that my ethical choices were always aimed at doing no harm to others and allowing myself the personal freedom necessary to continue in my own direction. No existing law would grant that justification, but from the observation point I had available at that moment, I could see and feel the complete redemption of each of my decisions.

It is difficult to describe how I was able to follow the intricacy of thoughts that spanned the course of my life. It was something I never thought possible, but it turned out that each second of my life was recorded in my consciousness, together with all my feelings and observations. The process took place of its own volition, and I just attended it with my mind, much to my own astonishment. Notably, there were only a few leading threads of thought. Like long serpents, they weaved through situations appearing in a sequential order. Each thread began with my earliest memories of observations and decision making, then was often modified by circumstances, branching out at some points to collect events and new experiences that also needed conclusions. Eventually, all those conclusions joined the original thought, the one that had begun the process. That was the general system I observed. It would take an extremely long time to describe each thought as it evolved in time, but I was able to perceive it in its full, complex meaning within seconds. Together with images, the initial thoughts appeared and took me all the way through my lifetime, up to the present moment.

One of the threads I followed was the decision I made when I was shocked by the pain caused to my childhood dog, the dachshund, by my actions. That vow to never again hurt anything solidified into a stance that determined my future choices, because of that initial truth I wanted to preserve. It shaped my later emotional approach to a variety of situations that chronologically ran through my mind and reminded me how I acted and what consequences my actions brought. As a result of that one decision, I did not fight back in situations when I should have protected myself. I was reminded of that as the images and associated thoughts ran through my mind, but the process was not about moral or reasonable right and wrong, nor was it for any personal benefit. It was really about those initial thoughts, that developed into feelings, opinions, stances, and conclusions that created who I was. The result of these thoughts now existed as a building block of my personality. I saw how my relationship with my mother, school, thoughts about my father, my love for my boyfriend and my daughter, my approach to work, money, art, sex, and adventure, all belonged to a string of thought and that each moment shaped who I had become. Now, I was able to watch them one by one and follow their development until they were carried into the present. Exactly at the moment that the thought I followed reached the present, it would be explained completely to me and, upon that very moment, it would simply vanish! Within just a few minutes, I had relived all the events of my life, recalled my exact thoughts and their development, and was able to see the chain of events and decisions as something that brought me to where I was at that moment. During the entire event, I remained completely aware of what was going on.

The thoughts in that process could be compared to bubbles of oxygen in water, traveling up, reaching the surface, and subsequently vanishing. I saw my life in detail, comprehended every second, and everything became very clear. At that point, I realized my life was resolved! There were no more questions or doubts. There were no thoughts lingering in my mind. They all came to their final stage and dispersed.

Now I could observe my new thoughts as they came up, they were just a few, connected with my observation of the process. I noticed that those thoughts met with the same destiny: evanescence. My mind was resolving them on its own, with me just watching. The thoughts again vanished one after another, as I felt my consciousness rapidly transforming.

My whole identity began to shift. The shield of identity, who I thought I was, became obsolete. I saw it separating from me, disintegrating in one slow, sweeping motion. It felt like a stiff, thick shell of dried-up, but heavy mud was suddenly shaken off my body. I could see it: it was dark gray but the motion seemed to alter the substance of mud. As it was falling off of my body, it came to look more like a dense, almost solid smoke, dissolving into nothingness. The quick dissolution of my identity was something that I felt physically. What used to be an integral part of me, detached and completely fell apart, then disappeared. The realization came with a sudden, tremendous release and lightness. That what I *was not* was gone! Magic had happened, and I had experienced it. There was no longer any need to label myself; I knew I existed in my full capacity, with my mind conscious of the changes taking place.

That experience taught me that it is fully possible for a mind to follow one thought at a time, observe its development, and reach a destination of resolution. In the end of the process, the thought, now completely clear in meaning, function, and logic, just disappears. Now, I could do it at will with any thought, and I knew the result would be the same: clarity and exponential expansion of mental capacity. I also realized that the vanishing of a thought would not end in the loss of it. The resulting feeling is a gain of light and clarity.

I now had access to all my thoughts as they freely appeared

in my mind. The scope of my mental vision became unlimited, and I felt no more need to find out who I was. I did not need to be anybody or to think of myself as somebody. The freedom of my existence was completely mine and, after seeing through its outer shell, I had nothing left to prove. Inside me, there was a liberated self, engaged in watching my own passage into something I had no name for at the time. I just knew I did not need to bother with myself and my problems anymore. I had no more problems. I realized that what was gone was the ego and now my individual consciousness was present and observing.

I remembered how horrible I had felt just moments before and how difficult I thought my life was. I used to be haunted by guilt and regrets, lingering in darkness, lost on a dead-end street. I ventured to the end of the road and could not find a way out, but then that incredible thing happened.

I quickly realized with full clarity that the miracle that just took place, was not reserved for me alone. I did not see myself as someone special, chosen to receive this. Oh, no, not at all. I knew I was not the only one. This condition is of universal potential and exists in everyone. I joyfully said to myself, "If this happened to me, it can happen to everybody!" Each of us owns the same mechanism that can transcend a complex life full of emotional and mental traps into a pure, perfectly functioning, intelligent existence. In that state problems can be resolved by simple focus of mind, and we can get answers by calmly but eagerly reaching for them by application of infallible reasoning. Yes! If it happened to me, it really can happen to anyone.

As the process took place in me, I felt more joy and lightness. I could perceive an infinity of concepts readily accessible all the time, and that there is no question that needs to remain unanswered. My mind opened with full awareness and could investigate any chosen issue down to its final resolution. Correctness of the investigation was absolute, and my mind worked perfectly. I knew I could use it to solve any problem, but at that moment, there was nothing left to solve. After experiencing and comprehending that capacity of my mind, there was no need to experiment with it anymore.

"I realized with full clarity that the miracle which just took place, was not reserved for me alone."

My attention shifted to focus on further observation of the process. All along I sensed the presence of the light, but it was no longer a rainbow. As I recognized the daytime glow coming from the window, I also saw radiance around me. At first, it was more like a milky, whitish light, but slowly tiny speckles of pale gold started to appear in it, growing brighter and more golden. I saw and felt myself lifting, levitating above the bottom of the tub, while the golden speckles fell on me and began to flow through me. I became weightless and joyous, and all around me, glowing, bright gold light flowed down in the form of dense, small, sparkling flakes. By then I could feel clearly that what was happening, was being given to me as some kind of surprising gift. I was being showered with gold light. My whole being became just abundant, ecstatic joy. I started to feel fully supported, held by the gold light and completely taken care of. There was nothing left to be afraid of in life. As the shimmering shower continued, I could not have been more elated. Having never before asked for anything like that or ever thought it possible, I could only receive that generous gift with full gratefulness, regardless of its origins. The sense of completeness that entered me after the bundle of thoughts vanished was now reinforced by some kind of a presence that I had started to feel nearby. I no longer thought anything; I just observed with full attention, completely aware, and when another realm opened, I knew I had entered the next state.

Again, I was alone in the bathroom of the empty house, only about fifteen minutes beyond experiencing suicidal urges, feeling deeply unhappy and hopeless. Now, I was joyous and ecstatic, bathing in the golden light, feeling a caring, knowing presence around me. I was not alone. Someone was near me. I could not see anyone, but I had a distinct sense that an entity was there. I felt its closeness more every second, and it felt wonderful. It was beautifully attractive and safe, and the energy flowing my way was definitely a giving one.

I observed how slowly and gently but without any hesitation, the presence took hold of me. I swayed toward it without control, but control was not needed. It felt like I was falling in love without any intention of turning back. Eventually, in a very distinct moment, I felt my heart being gripped with tactile sensation. I did not imagine it; I actually experienced it.

I could never have even dreamed what happened next, when the presence bestowed its love on me. I knew that I had always, somewhere deep inside, hoped and blindly searched for that love, but I had never been able to imagine it.

When I experienced the disintegration of thoughts and the shedding of ego, I knew I'd read about it somewhere before, but back then, I did not believe it was possible or true, and I could not relate to it. What happened in the next stage, though, was something I'd never read or heard about. Suddenly, that loving presence reached for and took me. It did not just love me from the heart but in every way, even a sensually satisfying one. A physical, sexual sensation was not manifested, but the orgasmic transcendence was felt in my whole being. The presence reached all the way into my heart, with true love, and an overwhelming, unmistakable sense of fulfillment took me over.

I fell in love completely in that instant. I felt all of me was now being loved madly and ecstatically, and I was madly and ecstatically in love with that Presence who loved me. I knew it was a forever feeling, a love that was complete, fulfilled, and real. It was more real than any love I had ever felt before. My heart was reached, and there was no distance between my lover and me. There was nothing but love, and I lived in it, basked in it. I was loved truly and I loved truly, leaving nothing behind. It was all love, in every way, not just a sweet, beautiful feeling but also a passionate fire. It was crazy love, a love like the first, the grandest love I could ever imagine and more. The Presence knew me intimately, all the way to my core, my every thought, every emotion, and completely loved me; mind, body, and soul. I felt it strongly, and I had no doubts about it. I knew I was not dreaming. I knew where I was and what was going on; I was very present. There was no error, and it felt like the target was hit. It was me the Presence was in love with, and I was in love with the Presence. I knew that feeling would never go away. It was there for good, forever. It had finally happened: Love had found me, and I had found it. We recognized each other fully, and nothing could ever destroy that eternal love we shared. I was home forever. Nothing was given up, everything was gained.

I bathed in the love I received and the love I happily gave, enjoying it with all my being. The ecstasy felt endless, and the realization of it was endless. At the same time, I knew that although it was given to me intimately and exclusively, that love is there for every being all the time. All beings are loved eternally, ecstatically, beautifully, and even madly. Love is there in all moments for everyone to receive, just as we are, in any state and any circumstance, at any time.

The space and colors surrounding me were light and gentle, flowing, translucent greens and pinks of infinite depths. I received that amazing love from my true, eternal partner, and I was filled with it. I was free to love, right to love, and full of love for the whole world. I knew that was what I came here to do: to give love endlessly, just as it had been given to me. The preciousness of that realization became sacred. With my whole being, I held that sacred love as the meaning of my life, as the meaning of all life...

"I started to think about the problems of the world, about how blinded we are by the material reality; how, because of that, we do not feel the love that can truly make everyone feel happy and satisfied."

Realizing the fulfillment I had just received, I rested peacefully and quietly. With delight, I began to send my abundant love to all troubled people, to beings who were living their lives while feeling unloved. It happened naturally, without any conscious consideration. My heart poured out love. As that took place and I witnessed it, I eventually comprehended that it was precisely what Buddha and Jesus taught and did. Love! Now, I understood why! Now, I knew that secret. They had received that same love and spent their lifetimes giving it and teaching it. My intuitive, idealistic visions and longings that had always been the core of my attitude toward life were sometimes pushed away by bad experiences, but they were not mere delusions. My desire for peace and love in the world was not just a naïve, silly fantasy of an inexperienced youth. It is not a shortcoming, a handicap that can be easily exploited by others to their advantage, like some people warned while I was growing up. Rather, that love is the wisest, deepest truth of life. I understood that Buddhism is not impractical wisdom but a most evolved teaching. The realms beyond the material world are more important than what we see with our physical eyes. That is where the essence of life is formed, and we should all reach for that wisdom by creating our lives on Earth according to those principles, just like Buddha and Jesus taught. I started to think about the problems of the world, about how blinded we are by the material reality; how, because of that, we do not feel the love that can truly make everyone feel happy and satisfied. We are convinced that personal love between two people is the only real love. We suffer from unrequited love or from loss of love. We pursue ideal sexual love with a desired partner. We place high importance on finding love in another person, and we naturally strive for that fulfillment. I am not saying that what we do is wrong, but it is good to know, that all the while, the true, real love we seek, that forever fulfilling love, is something that comes from another dimension of perception. Many problems persist because we do not know that each of us is eternally loved in the deepest, most intimate and profound way. We are too busy, attached to our physical, emotional, and mental dimensions to feel that love. Coming to these realizations filled me with a loving sense of compassion for all living beings who suffer and live in ignorance of the truth that ends suffering.

By the time I experienced the revelation about love, I was no longer concerned with my own life. All possible issues were completely resolved in the previous stage, at the point of dissolution of ego, which is nothing more than a conglomerate of thoughts. All my potential needs and desires were fulfilled in surplus, and I was united in love with the real source of love. Now personally fulfilled, I was able to see, clearly and lovingly, the rest of humanity, all the people and their problems and suffering, and I knew that I had been given wisdom that could help the world. "This is what it is all about!" I thought. "This is it!"

As I peacefully dwelled in that certainty and humbly came to terms with its magnitude, I noticed with surprise that the air around me started to slowly fill with sound. It startled me at first, and I thought how unusual it was that anyone would play loud music in the house in the middle of the day. I quickly realized there was no music anywhere in the house, but just around me. The sound slowly grew louder, and I noticed how delightful it was. A quiet murmur in a low tone soon sounded like a choir of hundreds of voices echoing from some far, far distance and coming closer in waves. The music was full, as if a monumental, heavenly orchestra surrounded me. It appeared together with a blue air that gradually got more intense and continued to darken everything around me, making me focus only on the music and nothing else. The depth of the tones was majestic. There were many layers to the sound. The choir of incredibly spectacular, angelic voices weaved into a captivating harmony... I heard a live ocean of sounds reverberating and harmonizing in the most spellbinding sequences, sung by voices in wide ranges, at frequencies that stretched beyond human capability. I listened in total awe, and although I already felt so high and ecstatic, the music somehow took me higher. I was swaying, entranced, mesmerized.

"I received greetings and was acknowledged, and I could access an immense depth of information if I so desired."

A while later, as the music continued, I noticed shapes coming out of the darkness. In my view, two figures scrolled down in front of me, but it looked like there were more at the periphery of my vision. The images appeared out of the beautiful deep blue, and the figures directly in front of me became illuminated, allowing me to more easily see their features. They passed slowly, and as each reached my eye level, I received a bow and a direct, deep gaze, forming the foundation of a connection. I could tell I was familiar with some of them, while I was not sure about the others. I sensed that these figures knew me, and I could tell that they were well aware of my present condition, that I was in the process of recognizing and dwelling in the other dimensions of existence. Although they almost looked like images, they were actual, real individuals who made real contact with me. I accepted their greetings and understood their appearance to be an introduction to their realm. They were the carriers of the sound, but those I saw were just a small part of that grand choir. While this took place, I had no words for what was going on, but at the same time, I knew it without words. As they introduced themselves to me one after another, I heard some of their names. They kept on descending at a constant, slow pace. At that moment, their individuality did not matter, nor did mine. The established connection was about the purpose of their work and the purpose of my passage and understanding. I got their message. The knowledge I was given was shared knowledge, guarded by those who received it and I became one of them.

Connection with each individual was very engaging and they also communicated with me as a group. I received greetings and was acknowledged, and I could access an immense depth of information if I so desired.

Humbly and with reverence I watched the figures slowly fade into the darkness when another stage of my transition began, yet another vision that I did not understand at first. On the deep purple, cosmic background, I saw many thin, straight, green lines. They traveled in four directions, seemed to cross quite evenly, and appeared to go on into infinity. I had no idea what it was. The image did not remind me of my breakthrough into the abstract dimension four years prior. This situation was different. I focused on it and proceeded to work towards an understanding. Since the dissolution of past thoughts during the earlier stage, my mind was free and sharp. I felt a natural clarity, a certainty that I could under-stand anything. The state of my mind was exceptional. The points where some lines intersected were marked with small and strong, bright neon green and blue lights. Each had an even brighter center, warmer green turning to clean yellow and light pink, with the bright white light in the middle. The little lights appeared to be pulsating softly and their intensity was changing. In general, the light points looked very similar,

were equally distanced from one another, and infinite num-
bers of them were disappearing into perspective with thin,
green laser lines shimmering in darkness. There was motion
in the image, action. The energy I felt from the vision seemed
familiar, though I could not place why. As I watched a little
longer, it finally came to me: I was looking at the matrix of
creation! The light points indicated where coded information
about each life, past and future, was created and recorded.
They were the sources of individual lives. Followed by a sense
of intrigue, a question quickly formed in my mind: "Is my life
in there as well?" Although the matrix was infinitely huge, I
hovered over it easily. After a relatively short search, I came
upon one of the points, one I knew was my own essence.
"Here I am! My life is in that tiny capsule. It is that tiny green
light"... I came to know, feeling moved and amazed. The substance of each life, already designed and completed with all
the events, thoughts, deeds, and feelings was incubating right
there, on that grid of the green lines. I saw something that
was created beyond the frame of time we are accustomed to
looking at. The image was already there before we could see
it or identify it. It existed in another dimension.

At that moment, I realized and saw clearly that what we see
as time is an illusion, merely a measure with a function in
our experience of life. We depend on it for our concepts of
reality. Otherwise, time does not exist. What we think of as
our future has already happened. Each of us has a life that has
already happened, in the past and in the future. It was decided
upon in the visionary dimension that can be entered under

some circumstances, as when it happened to me. What we presume to be our own decisions and moves, deeds and merits are not really ours in the sense that a different dimension of our perception created them, different than the one in which we dwell most of the time and the one of which we are most conscious of. Each second of our lives, of everyone's life, is completely done, already decided on beforehand. We spend our lives just chasing our shadows, rushing into what is unknown to us but, in truth, it all has already happened.

"It was inside of me, nothing but the brilliant, immense, tremendous realization that eventually formed into a statement."

When all that became clear, a surging new wave of yet more expanded and deeper consciousness arose in me. My initial conclusion that the matrix of creation and all lives have a coded destiny that is simply formulated on a grid was a rather somber discovery, but it would quickly become of minimal importance. Within a split second, it was replaced by an eruption of conscious energy that could not be described by words. Its appearance was not external. It was not a vision. It was inside of me, nothing but the brilliant, immense, tremendous realization that eventually formed into a statement. The magnitude of it was beyond anything I had ever experienced or imagined before. It took over all my previous realizations in the process. In a silent, atomic explosion I arose from the inside, a free and boundless being.

Statement "I AM" came from the depths of my existence. It

is practically impossible to describe that realization, but it felt like something immense emerged and spoke, and there was no way to add anything to it. I remained in the state of that glorious recognition for a while. It was a state of acute awareness. I knew exactly where I was and who I was. I also knew exactly how the whole process started and how it had developed. None of my past was in any way blurred or forgotten. I was not taken from my surroundings and transported anywhere. All that I was up until that point, I still was. The transcendence of thoughts and the shedding of the shell of identity that followed were in my constant awareness as well. I was loved, and I was loving deeply. The understanding of illusion of time and material reality was comprehended with lucidity and precision, and such was my present state. The plain, austere bathroom was still the same, and I was still sitting in the old-fashioned tub. Daylight seeped through the vines outside the window. It was about 2:50 p.m. on March 10, 1992, in Los Angeles. The phenomena did not contradict one another because I was in a state of full awareness and apprehension. I saw through all the dimensions at once. Still, unbelievably so, all of that was a setting for yet another new realization.

My existence presented itself on the background of eons of time, throughout the lifetimes. It seemed to me there was nothing extraordinary about it; it was only the truth, finally revealed in full liberation. My scope of vision widened into timeless peripheries, encompassing my being as a single unit of awareness that existed independently of any measure. The illusion of the material world became thoroughly clear, and

the true me - the soul, the Self - was finally free, forever released from any earthly concerns. I realized that the sense of
individual identity stays with the soul throughout all lifetimes
and that all souls carry similar characteristics.

The nature of what I called an eruption of conscious energy
led to the next stage, allowing me a very particular discernment. In turn, that brought about another astounding realization. At first, I noticed that soul, while timeless, appears
on the background of physical reality as a creator of itself, in
a burst of what I describe as wakeful, breathless creative im-
pulse. That moment of discernment illuminated my very reason for being. I finally understood why, throughout my whole
life, my truest instinctive desire was to focus on creating. It
became completely clear that the urge I had been feeling all
my life, the deep, irresistible pull into the creative process, is
the intrinsic nature of all souls.

All the pains of mortal life were worth that clarification. I
reached the depth of understanding which is the core of our
existence and felt the indescribable magnitude of the revealed
truth.

Following the observation about the soul creating itself, a
new discovery became clear: The whole of our existence on
every level comes into being continually in an outpouring of
that blissfully sublime, yet unimaginably potent force. It is a
spark, a thought so powerful that it can manifest on all levels
of existence. All is created simultaneously, in every moment

anew, just by the energy of a thought. The sphere of thoughts is instantly comprehended and arranged into concepts that are, in that state, still abstract. My sudden breakthrough from four years before reached into that sphere of conceptual, live creation, and I finally realized what had happened then. I existed in that sphere again, this time clearly one of the thoughts, observing my own becoming.

My mind, in its inherent mode of exploring further, began wondering what gives soul the energy to create itself, when the next question eagerly appeared: "What creates all of life?" The answer was doubtless and, as I thoroughly saw into it, my mind was blown, yet again.

"The whole of our existence on every level comes into being continually in an outpouring of that blissfully sublime, yet unimaginably potent force."

Inspiration. I naturally grasped that thought and at once became it. I felt the expansion of my awareness in an instant, reaching everywhere. I perceived how, in the actuality of the deed, I AM the creator in the moment of creating. I was God, and I connected with God in omnipresent lucidity and bliss. It was not only the understanding that I was created by consciousness and was consciousness; it was also clear that I created that consciousness. At that moment, anything that could be still further observed and comprehended was flushed away by the brightest light that suddenly and completely engulfed me. I tried to think and make more conclusions, I was soaring like a comet in that boundless illumination to find more thoughts, but it was just not possible. Suddenly, there was not a single thought left. There was only very bright light.

The state of full consciousness exists in the absence of all thought: not only the strategic thoughts which revolve around our material and personal existence, but also the intellectual faculty of observing and witnessing is no longer called for. I knew I was creating myself and the whole world. Just by being in the state of constant, inexhaustible inspiration, in effortless and peaceful ecstasy of potential creation, all life is realized. I say "potential" because that's the essence of consciousness, the energy that creates unlimited potential. What we experience as our life is a result of our multidimensional perceptions.

Each of the previous stages was eventful in the sense that a describable transition took place. The stage of union with God had no other attributes but light and blissful awareness: no thoughts, no changes, no time. It was not possible to think or measure anything, yet the awareness was absolute, beyond any knowledge. I dwelled in the completion of eternity. The precious sacredness that was initiated with the discovery of boundless, ever-present love was carried to the utmost state of unity and peace in full capacity of being.

Immediately After The Experience

What happened was given to me, and I had no control over any of the process, other than to make sure I was present to observe it. I knew I had no choice whether I would go through it or not. When the process was complete, I just sat motionless, until I knew it was time to get up and get out of the tub. I had no idea how long the whole thing took, but when I was putting my clothes back on and looking around the bathroom, recognizing my environment as the same yet completely new, I noticed that the cockroach was still there. It was now high up on the wall, almost to the ceiling. When I saw it again after my experience, I found significance in it. The cockroach no longer repulsed me; I felt good about it being there, living its simple and magical life. I was happy to see it and just let it be. I knew it was in the caring hands of the Presence - the ultimate consciousness, together with everything else. All was clear, but I could not find words for anything.

"In place of any mental analysis of what happened, I had only awe and total reverence."

I went upstairs to my studio. I was acutely aware what happened, but it was impossible to express, my mind was blown. The lid was blown off the top of my head, and I did not want or need to think. I was speechless, but that was fine because I did not want to speak to anyone anyway. I no longer had a program to follow, a plan to realize, or a dream to fulfill. I knew I was going to do something, even if I wasn't sure what it was. I did not care, because I was free. I could laugh and cry and do nothing, for whatever I did was already complete.

In place of any mental analysis of what happened, I had only awe and total reverence. The scope of what I went through was beyond any possible rationalization. I was much more than amazed and wonderstruck. The recognition of the un-believable greatness demanded nothing short of complete de-votion and surrender. "This is how religions are born," I said to myself.

Days Later

Ten days after my experience, I still had not spoken to any-one. There was no need. From my studio in the MacArthur Park area, I walked to West Hollywood. I knew the city but re-alized that I'd never really been there before. I did not know how to be there. I used to walk just like I did now, but I was never completely present. Before, there was always a distance between me and everything else, a question, a consideration, a doubt, and a fog of uncertainty. The world used to exist outside me, it was not mine. I used to want pieces of it, the pieces I liked and pieces I thought I could not live without. I used to reach for what I thought I rightfully deserved and push away what I did not want. I used to strategize, plan, and assume. When I got what I wanted, I felt satisfied; when I didn't, I felt frustrated. I used to position myself and approach people and situations because that was what I needed to do.

All those stipulations and maneuvers stood in the way of me seeing clearly. Now, I could see myself as being present and the world was mine. All mine. Not in the sense of ownership but in the sense of identity. I was the world. At the same time, I was physically standing on the corner of Santa Monica and La Cienega, observing the reality around me, present. Existence kept continuing forever... I could feel eternity. I was smiling. I clearly felt I came down to the ground and touched it. I knew I finally landed. I watched the endless show fleeting in front of me, people busy with their lives, rushing somewhere, everybody passing me by, but they are all me. "All is me and I love it all." The present moment was motionless, yet I was moving somewhere. I didn't know how to describe what happened to me, but I knew what happened. I was still in the place when the light hit me ten days earlier, except now I was out on the street, feeling the same and being the same as when I realized I created it all. The constant, stable, eternal sense of realization, completion and freedom, happiness and peace made me chuckle from time to time.

To this day, even as I write this, that state is present. It is beyond any external circumstances. There is no going back from it because it is not a body or mind thing, although it transforms mind and body as well. That day, on the streets of L.A., to analyze what happened and gain distance from it was not what I wanted. I lived it and felt it naturally. The experience started to settle into my system, making me open and vulnerable like a child who couldn't talk yet... but that was fine. Every second was memorable, every little moment worthwhile. "This is how it always is", I said to myself. "This is how precious and dear everything always is." Besides feeling pure, organic love for everything, there was another theme that intrigued me, but it was very vague. I could perceive it only from the same viewpoint which was opened to me during the awakening process, from the position of observer. This theme was more in depth about the nature of life and direct formulation of my experience in an understandable way, while my experience still felt very alive, but I had become physically removed from it by time and space.

By now, I had a good idea that the several minutes the process lasted contained information that could take a very, very long time to describe, if describing it was even possible. I could not even find words for it yet! Being a visual artist, it is images that are always coming to my mind first when I want to say something, which often makes the task of explaining something verbally, difficult. Since there was no comparison to anything I had experienced before or anything I ever knew about, I had to let go of my desire to verbalize it right away and just keep on watching it with my eyes wide open, grateful and humble, still in a state actualized by the experience. I needed much more time to gather my impressions and recall everything in an accessible form. In the meantime, not knowing where I was going, I was open for anything. I was walking somewhere...

"The large billboard up above and a trashcan by the

entrance to the mall were nothing but the pure and lucid breath of the divinity."

I looked around at life, movements, people, cars, the sky, the buildings, and the streets. I knew those streets, I had been there many times before. Now, I was walking without a plan, feeling completely free. Besides the view I was used to, I could see something else in between objects, other people, and me. It was the space, the air... I knew it was full of what I had realized ten days before. That, which permeated everything I saw. It was in the palm trees, in the wind that gently caressed the leaves. The sky was full of it, as was the smoggy L.A. haze. The large billboard up above and a trashcan by the entrance to the mall were nothing but the pure and lucid breath of the divinity. The door of a restaurant held it, it was in the sudden squeal of car brakes. It was in me and I knew, once I saw it, that nothing would ever be the same again.

Ramana Maharshi

"I felt the fulfillment of that recognition in a burst of love so powerful, I swayed and melted from the impact."

I found myself approaching a bookstore called the "Bodhi Tree". The books I usually read were books about art and I could find them there. I liked the unique collection that the bookstore had. However, this time, I was not looking for an art book. I did not know why I was entering the store, but it felt good. I did not think I wanted to find references to my experience, that idea had not become clear in my mind, I was just wandering. The material world was such a tiny fragment of what I had experienced and I was now relating to it in a new way. Ultimately, it did not matter what I knew or wanted, because my feet took me to an unfamiliar room full of bookshelves loaded with hundreds of books. I began to feel a bit disoriented because I had no idea what I was looking for. My feet walked over to a certain shelf without any hesitation, I pulled a book from a row of many. In my hands was a medium size book with a dark orange fabric cover.

I opened it with a tinge of doubt. On one of the first pages there was a photograph of a man's face. I looked at it. My eyes were immediately drawn unto his. My jaw dropped as I recognized the gaze. My whole body became covered in goose bumps. I felt the fulfillment of that recognition in a burst of love so powerful, I swayed and melted from the impact. My mind experienced yet another new blow. "Yes, this is it!" The connection was made, and a shared understanding passed from his eyes to mine. That same love, that same union I received, shone in his eyes. I looked at his beautiful face, his smile. I recognized with full certainty he'd had the same experience. I could read in his eyes that he knew the same thing I did, I felt it with my whole being. I knew that he had appeared, ten days after the event, as a confirmation of my experience. Tears welled in my eyes, and I could not stop them from rolling down my face. I bowed my head and instinctively joined my hands in gratitude. "Thank you, thank you, thank you!" The gift of his presence was unmistakable. I read his name: Ramana Maharshi. The book was published in India and contained transcriptions of his conversations with disciples and visitors over a span of years. I did not know if I was going to read the book, but I had to get it because of the picture alone, because of the sense of recognition that I found in his eyes. I was not ready to superimpose any existing knowledge on top of my experience. I knew the experience came from the subtle sphere of cognition, and the link to that sphere was delicate. I needed to keep that union with the supernatural alive, and I did not want to clutter it with any external information. I wanted to cultivate it, make it stronger on my own.

For that reason, I very carefully approached the book later that year. It contained a series of questions and answers as recorded by his devoted disciples. Ramana Maharshi had his experience when he was 16 years old. He spent many years contemplating it afterwards. His teachings are more about the essence of spiritual enlightenment and less about the process of getting there. His exquisite choice of words helped me get over my initial speechlessness, but my speechlessness was also validated, since his main method of teaching was through silence. At the time, in 1992, not many people world-wide knew about Ramana Maharshi. These days, however, he is rightfully considered one of the most prominent spiritual teachers.

CHAPTER III: LIFE AFTER THE EXPERIENCE

Hawaii

Within a month of my experience, many things happened. At a get-together with some friends, I tried to explain what had happened to me. Although they were open-minded and bright people, and artists like me, I seemed unable to get my message across to them, at least not in a way that allowed for clear understanding. I was only met with silent stares that meant my friends just did not know what to say. That encounter made it clear to me that I might very well be left on my own with my discovery, and the only humans who could have had the potential to relate were inaccessible; Ramana Maharshi, Buddha, Jesus or the individuals who appeared during my experience. I accepted this, but I also knew that whatever had happened was not over and I was not going to live the same life that I had lived before. I'd always been quite sensitive, but now I was hypersensitive. I could feel people from a distance and I could sense what they were thinking. In a not-so-great part of Los Angeles where I was living, police choppers hovered over my head day and night, in search of criminals and drug traffickers, my landlady's dogs barked nonstop, and I was constantly surrounded by chaos. It was nothing new, but I needed change. I did not know how that change would present itself, but I was ready for it.

My landlady, whom I spoke to briefly, albeit without mentioning anything about my experience, suggested that I take a Hawaiian vacation. I had never been to Hawaii before or ever thought much about it, but it just so happened that a few days later I heard from an acquaintance of mine who was heading to Hawaii for a ten-day trip. He invited me to join him. Somehow, I sold a painting just in time to earn a little money for the trip. Once we arrived in Honolulu, I felt a strong urge to head to Maui. I had no idea why, but the need was overwhelming. My friend insisted on exactly three days on each island, like any proper tourist would, but I did not want to wait. We agreed to separate and I used my meager financial resources to get a one-way ticket to Maui.

I rented a car at the airport and, led strictly by intuition, without looking at maps or asking for directions, I drove to Paia, a little village about thirteen miles from Kahului, a windsurfing hangout. I went to a coffee shop for a bite to eat, and sat there wondering what I should do next. The busy little eatery had a friendly atmosphere. I was not sure why or how, but it felt as if I was going to meet someone at any given moment. A short while later, that was precisely what happened.

A man approached and engaged me in conversation. One of the first things he asked me was, "What are your spiritual views?" At that moment, I knew I was in the right place. The people there had the same interests as I did, and it was easy to communicate with them. A couple of weeks later, I wrote in my very inconsistent diary, "Maui is my home." I stayed on Maui for two years. There, I could finally allow my experience to settle within me. The tropical jungle and the ocean knew what I was doing and welcomed me home.

People seemed to gather around me wherever I went, as if drawn in by my energy. I realized I was needed, but after several weeks of so much attention and very little privacy, especially since I stayed with new friends in various parts of the island, the interest that I was generating exhausted me. I yearned for more private accommodations. Sometime around my third week on Maui I got, almost literally, kidnapped by an awesome new friend, who became my boyfriend and we lived together in his house. I felt completely and beautifully taken care of.

Still, there was much to consider and to come to terms with. My experience, which lasted only several minutes, required years of contemplation. The contemplation is still going on and, as far as I understand, it is a process that will never end. Practicing contemplation is a necessary part of the evolution of the soul. My life changed completely, but my general direction remained the same, and the truth was and still is my main interest in life. Art was still my method of expression and communication, but now, I was no longer troubled with the past or future or overwhelmed by the present. I just continued my life. I did not work on my nonobjective paintings but spent a lot of time contemplating in peace. I knew life was going on around me. Like everyone else, I was involved in many different situations, and there were people around. I had friends and plans for the future, but I faced it all from a different perspective.

I naturally felt one with everything, constantly in the here and now. At the same time, I realized we all live in a fairytale (even if it is not always a pleasant one), so things can always change and everything is possible. On Maui, I spent most of the time in nature, in love with it. I met wonderful, happy, beautiful people. I saw rainbows and auras around some, and heard angelic voices singing. Being around those who were also on a conscious spiritual path was a great comfort to me, especially since I was so sensitive and psychically attuned. When I needed something, I visualized it. Some of those visualizations came to fruition quickly, while others took longer. Others are still to manifest, but I am not worried about it.

As wonderful as it all was, I still faced challenges. Decisions were easier, though, and I was much calmer in general, because I knew that I belong to the world and can trust the universe.

> **"Life's ups and downs were still there, but they existed in the background of the ever-present sense of love, peace, and positivity of every situation."**

I took time to describe the process I went through, if only for my own records. I saw clearly that it consisted of seven distinguished stages. The figures who visited me while I was surrounded by music were the ascended masters, and they acknowledged my perception into the dimension of communication and akashic records. Slowly, I began to put together a record of my experience in the context of what was already known on the subject. I realized I had experienced a full, complete kundalini rising. I found that the download of information I received was immeasurably greater than anything I could ever learn in one lifetime. A lot of it could not be translated to words. The realization was fully there, but I needed time to contemplate it and to find the words to describe it. It took a long time to create a proper account of the process and to determine the meaning of the transformation I went through.

All the stagnant energy that had been making me feel weak and heavy was chased away during the kundalini rising process. The emotional burden connected to my relationship with my mother and inability to deal with pain relating to problems, which were gnawing at me before, had all disappeared. My daughter was to spend her summer vacation with me on Maui, and I talked to my mother on the phone about it. I briefly mentioned my experience. She laughed at me and quickly commented, "You've read too many books," but she could no longer upset me. I had no need to prove anything, as I had become aware that we each live our own destinies. Unless we can see through it, we can't really change the way we are. My mother never wanted or believed in change, so she remained as she was. All I could do was be understanding and compassionate about her condition. Unconditional love and care took place of the painful emotional connection from the past.

I was so much stronger, and my physical energy seemed inexhaustible. Inside, I continually felt joy and peaceful exuberance. I did not have to think about it; it just was that way. Life's ups and downs were still there, but they existed in the background of the ever-present sense of love, peace, and positivity of every situation.

My boyfriend graciously took me to Poland, so I could meet with my father and spend four meaningful hours with him. It was very important to me and I think to him as well. The bond with my father began to take shape now, after so many years of silence, and he answered many of my questions even before I asked them. He confessed to me that he had also felt traumatized by my mother while living with her. My father had a natural healing energy about him, and after retiring from theater, he spent time healing with his hands in the local church.

After a couple of years in Maui, the relationship with my boyfriend ended, and I moved back to L.A. Life seemed hard again, but I did not experience difficulties in the same way I did before. Rather than being depressed and overwhelmed by the turn of events, I felt strong and resourceful, even hopeful.

A few months later, I visited a friend in the Lake Tahoe area. I fell in love with the area and passionately got into skiing, fulfilling yet another dream. I eventually moved to the outskirts of Reno, Nevada, a city that is close to several ski resorts, and I became a ski bum. My physical energy continued to be abundant, and skiing almost daily became my spiritual practice. White snow was now my home and sky was my breath. The practice of a smooth, effective turn in the bumps and steeps was my affirmation of the joyous, ecstatic participation in life. The difficulty and danger of it was what I needed. "Don't let the fear take over," was my cautious motto. "Learn the technique"... Just like when working on my paintings in L.A. – focus was the key to my practice.

The experience didn't change me into a different person, but now I also knew for sure that I was much more than I thought I was, and I could always reach into the depth of my being to find guidance, support and fulfillment. It became clear that in every moment of my life I am an expression of the creator, and my practice is to chase away the ignorance of the ego and be one with the divine that took me in to be one with it. The basic wisdom I retained from the experience assured me that I needed to practice. For many years, I did it subconsciously, out of instinctive need, but now the practice has become conscious.

I did not want to go back to my career as an artist or play any important role, but I still painted and occasionally sold originals, prints, or cards. To supplement my income I still sometimes danced in the local nightclub. Skiing and hiking a lot led me to the invention of an exciting device for skiers and hikers, which I got patented. My sensitivity was still heightened and I both saw and heard invisible beings, especially in some spots in the mountains.

From the spirits of the Washoe Indians, I learned about a massacre that took place sometime around 1850. I did not know why they wanted to share the information with me but, a few years later, through a series of magical circumstances, I acquired my dream house, a tiny fixer-upper, perched on top of a hill overlooking the Sierra Nevada mountains and the resort where I ski. It was another desire completely fulfilled, a real home of my own, and a true retreat. I realized it was given to me by those same spirits who inhabit the ridges of the Slide Mountain and areas nearby. Their story needs to be told, and I promised I would do that, so I intend to write about it sometime soon. Part of my home became my art studio where I could get back to my nonobjective painting.

Throughout the years, not a day has gone by without my March 10 experience alive in my heart. It changed my life forever. It brought love, hope, and peace to even most difficult circumstances. It gave me the ability to witness instead of react. I started to use my capacity to understand instead of getting angry, to feel compassion instead of feeling victimized. Even if I did react, got angry, or felt victimized at the times, I knew it was only the result of a lack of practice.

I knew the solution is in me, not anywhere else. I focused increasingly on practice, something I will write more about in the next chapters.

IMMEDIATE CHANGES NOTICED AFTER THE EXPERIENCE

Changes caused by a full kundalini rising, for the sake of easier understanding, can be viewed as immediate and long-term transformations. The immediate ones were very apparent to me and did not require much investigation.

1. Inner Joy and Peace

As described above, from the moment the experience took place, nothing could erase the new emotional base that was created. Nothing could keep me down and negative emotions no longer had anything to adhere to. My emotional reactions to upsetting situations were completely present and fully felt, but after acknowledgment, they quickly vanished. Joy and happiness became the true, deep state, while all negative emotions were just short lived and dispersed without a trace.

2. Feeling Loved

Up until the day of my experience, it was not clear to me if I was loved. I think my grandmother loved me, but in our culture, as far as I know, it was not at all common to tell someone, "I love you," so I never heard her say it. I knew she cared about me. I also assumed my mother loved me, even if there were signs that it might have been otherwise. I felt pressure to earn her love by being the way she wanted me to be, but I was unsuccessful. The same happened later, in my relationship with my daughter's father. That relationship helped me discover that people can change and simply stop loving someone. It was also a cruel realization that things can end suddenly, against our own desire. From then on, I engaged in several relationships which would begin with falling in love and end with somebody either brokenhearted or at least a bit disillusioned. Very few of those relationships developed into something more profound, but those, again, would end one way or another. Then there was always the dream of a love-filled relationship and the hope that the next one would fulfill the dream.

During the most intimate moment of my kundalini experience, my heart was reached for and touched, and my whole being was infused with love. It was not a temporary love, based on conditions or circumstances. It did not come from another human being. Love does not cease; it is something I feel, know, and have forever. It is also sacred and untouchable, just like the kind of love I had dreamt about. I felt my heart was now beating to the rhythm of a blissful wave within me. I often sat in awe, marveling at the incredible feeling and the change it brought to my life. I laughed, cried, and thanked the Presence for letting me find myself, for allowing me to feel loved and in love. Since that moment, I've been able to reach that love anytime, and it is always there. Happily, many of us are able to reach it and we can all learn to dwell in love.

3. Loving The World

I have always loved the world and cherished life, but it was not always a happy love. Even with the base of my naturally enthusiastic approach to life when I was very young, my optimism faded and lessened in time. Knowing about the on-going hardships and problems endured by humans, and about progressing destruction of the environment was depressing. I felt I was not helping the world by failing in placing my artwork in public forums, and barely surviving from one week to the next. My own hardships lingered, and I was troubled by negative emotions. Just so I could afford to have my art studio, I was living in a poor section of L.A. I saw drugged-out prostitutes sleeping in the alley at all hours of the day and night and the crime in the area was rampant. The living conditions in my studio were hard. When I set out on my mission at the age of 19, I vowed to myself that I would not shy away from anything human, anything that could help me understand and succeed. Unfortunately, the human condition I observed gave rise to anger and helplessness. Yes, I always loved the world, but it became a tormented relationship. Not only was the world scary, but the perpetuation of misery seemed hopeless.

On the day of my experience, I was standing in the bathroom looking at a huge cockroach climbing a wall. Shortly after my experience, I saw the cockroach again, higher on the wall. There was nothing repulsive about it anymore. It was simply another creature living its own life, minding its own business. I knew it was loved, and I played an active part in letting it be that way. I left the bathroom feeling that everything was fine. I realized the feeling of love for the world was pouring out of me from the moment the presence touched my heart, and I understood what happened. It was not an urge to change all that seemed bad in the world but, rather, it was a feeling full of love and care for everything. The love in me opened with such great relief – I was free to love.

4. Release of Emotional Baggage

I described my life before the experience for several reasons. One was to present the amount of emotional burden I was carrying, starting from my earliest memories to the moment of my kundalini rising experience. I wrote about the times that affected me the most and made me develop in the way I did. We all carry baggage from the past. For some, it is heavier than mine, and others carry lighter weight. By the age of 35, my emotional baggage was so heavy that it was crushing me. Pain, resentment, a sense of loss, helplessness, and guilt oppressed me daily.

After the experience, those feelings were gone. Problems that had burdened me for years simply vanished, and I could think about them without attachment, without feeling the load of emotional pain dropping on me and keeping me down for long periods. At first, I did not even realize that freedom. I was constantly blown away, relishing my new life, feeling love and peace within. Thinking about the past was easy, and it did not trigger negative emotions. In their place, there was clarity and knowledge of what happened. Those stories were sealed with respect and compassion for all that took place and everyone that had been involved.

5. Different Way of Experiencing Negative Emotions

During my kundalini rising, I became aware of myself and my environment in a way that was incomparably more sensitive than ever before. That sensitivity stayed with me, and I began feeling everything more precisely. My range of emotions widened. Meeting with sad and unpleasant things did evoke negative emotions, but something changed. Once I could feel those emotions at their core, whether it was me reacting to something or someone nearby doing it, the emotions dissipated and were instantly replaced by feelings of love, compassion, and benevolence. The confirmation of love underlying all of life, the moment of remembrance of the truth, has been clearing negativity ever since.

6. The Magic of Being

Without thinking about it or actively trying to figure out reasons for it, my attitude toward life changed wonderfully. I felt love and knew all was created with love. There was no need for explanations to welcome life with wide-open arms; the words would come later.

I just lived and watched, keeping my life simple, and enjoying my solitude. In the past I sometimes used to seek company and entertainment to get away from my problems, if only for a time. Now, I had no unsolvable, massive problems and my time alone was joyous. Maui was a perfect place to go through the transition. I was in a continual state of gratitude and awe but also felt rather fragile because of my heightened sensitivity. I did not talk much, but I felt vibrations from plants, objects, people, and animals. Knowing that consciousness permeates everything, even every speck of dust, made life unfold in a miraculous way. The whole act of life began to exude unimaginable, magical greatness. Being has become a delight.

7. Reading People's Feelings and Thoughts

Although I've always intuitively perceived others' thoughts and feelings to some degree, after the kundalini rising, the intensity of that perception increased. I knew what was going on with somebody upon meeting them. Individual or even group energies were readable to me instantly, whether I interacted with them or not.

8. Seeing the Invisible

On top of a regular vision of reality, I was now able to experience other phenomena as well. I realized that there were invisible beings around me sometimes and I became aware of them. Most of the time, if I wanted to, I could see auras around people or unexpected colors around objects, but sometimes, I also heard voices giving me information.

About six months after my arrival on Maui, I was invited to a gathering on the beach, where a psychic from the Big Island was giving readings. Her name was Rainbow. None of my friends who were going knew who she was, and at the time, we were not even sure if she was a woman. We arrived in a huge, grassy area, with small groups of people spread all over. Since we were not looking for a reading and were there to simply enjoy a gathering of friends, we did not bother to even look around for her. A relaxing day ensued, and more friends showed up.

At some point, I stood up to take a look around, and I saw something interesting in the distance, a dome of translucent blue color, possibly about ten feet high. At first, I thought it was a huge tent and I was intrigued by the bright, intense blue hue of it and the fact that it was strangely transparent. I wanted to investigate it and asked a couple of my friends to take a walk with me. As we got closer to the curious structure, I saw rainbows swirling inside, like colorful ribbons floating in the breeze. There was a person sitting inside the dome. My friends had no idea that I saw the dome and the rainbows, but I watched the colored light dance until I reached the person who was sitting there. I could still feel the ethereal structure of the dome when I said, "Hello, Rainbow. I saw you in a blue dome with rainbows floating around you". Rainbow smiled and replied, "God bless you."

9. Knowledge About the Nature of God

My experience made me understand right away, that the true source of life - God, Brahman, Divine, or whichever other name is given to the ever-present absolute consciousness - is an incredible force not to be scared by and feared, as some religions have been teaching. It is the power of pure goodness, which is reaching out to us with true love.

PART THREE:

Seven Worlds
One Truth

CHAPTER IV: UNDERSTANDING

The incredible experience of kundalini rising has been described in so many ways, over thousands of years. It is impossible to present in words all the information that I received during my experience. However, it is possible to compare parts of my experience to the existing body of knowledge on kundalini rising and states of spiritual enlightenment, to help gain clarity on the phenomenon. Discussing it is a form of *sat-sang*. Sat-sang is a spiritual practice consisting of in person meetings, that translates to "gathering in truth."

WHAT IS SPIRITUAL ENLIGHTENMENT?

"Self-realization changes every aspect of our life, and it is a true state of eternal existence beyond any material evidence."

Spiritual enlightenment (self-realization) is the result of a process. Each of us has the potential to go through it, but whether it will happen in this lifetime depends on many factors. The whole process has not yet been scientifically proven, although we have been making huge progress in getting there. Whether discovered by science or not, it is a real, quite uniform development occurring in the person (body and mind) which leads to a new state of being. Human beings have been experiencing it for many millennia.

Spiritual enlightenment is not a philosophy. However, the way it has been interpreted by the ones who have experienced it, can be understood as philosophy or a system of wisdom. Knowledge about spiritual enlightenment has been shared in many forms: philosophical, religious, ritualistic, shamanistic, and mystical. It has been expressed through arts like poetry, music, dance, visual and performance arts. Only recently (for about the last 100 years), spiritual insights have been expressed in a pure art form, not belonging to any religion, philosophy, or cultural custom. I am talking about the birth of pure abstraction in visual art at the beginning of the 20th century and some forms of free jazz.

Spiritual enlightenment is an independent phenomenon. It does not come from any one cultural tradition, but it has been the inspiration for many cultures, as well as for many religions. It can happen to any human being, regardless of background, education, or social standing. The process is a strictly intimate, personal transcendence of one's consciousness through multidimensional spectrum of perceptions. An individual realizes one's true being (Self) as an eternal unit of awareness (soul) and ultimately perceives through and unites with what has been recognized as God or Divine, the source of all life. Enlightenment needs to be experienced in order for it to be fully understood by an individual. There is no mental substitute, it cannot be figured out or imagined beforehand. Final intellectual comprehension is one of the last stages of transition to an enlightened state. Self-realization changes every aspect of our life, and it is a true state of eternal existence beyond any material evidence.

In our history, since the beginning of first known civilizations, we have created religions and religious beliefs that stem from the spiritual enlightenment experience. All religions are concerned with trying to find ways of getting closer to God.

While in the West we have been historically taught obedience and worship of the unattainable qualities of God, Eastern religions like Hinduism, Buddhism, and Jainism prescribe various practices aimed at realizing the enlightened state of union with God. The greatest spiritual teachers have had the experience and it is the source of their wisdom. Spiritual practices have been followed by billions of people over the millennia, yet the experience of self-realization has not been a common occurrence. In recent years, the attainment of a spiritual fulfillment independent of religious doctrines has become an important quest all over the world. The nature of the phenomenon has never changed and the experience is available to everyone. The most important aspect of self-realization is the full recognition of the nature of what we call God, but the experience also creates a new being out of the person we thought we were. With right predispositions, the experience can happen spontaneously. There is no need for basal knowledge nor belief in God or spiritual enlightenment.

THE PROCESS THAT LEADS TO SPIRITUAL ENLIGHTENMENT

"Every incident of realizing an enlightened state is a result of a kundalini rising, but the stages of transition may not always be distinguishable with clarity."

Spiritual enlightenment comes to us. It happens. It is facilitated through the process called kundalini rising which needs to be complete to result in self-realization (spiritual enlightenment). Western civilization, mainly because of constraining dogmas and the political, economic, and cultural power of organized religions over the millennia, has not acknowledged this phenomenon as something potentially available to everyone. The signs of kundalini rising (revelations of all kinds relating to spiritual realms), were kept under the term "religious experience," reserved to church figures and people who accept formalized religions as ultimate truths. Having a spiritual experience without incorporating it into a local religious doctrine was once regarded as a bad thing. Today, we are much freer to reach for knowledge that helps with direct attainment of spiritual enlightenment.

In several Indian traditions, self-realization has been considered for millennia the worthiest goal in life. Many of the words used today to communicate the experience are either directly translated from ancient Sanskrit or used in their original form. *Kundalini* means "coiled one," but I have learned that it can also mean "fire." Both interpretations point at the basic character of the phenomenon. Kundalini is the latent force resting at the bottom of the spine, in the sacrum. It is our individual unit of consciousness. It is sometimes seen leaving the body, of a human or animal, at the time of death. It appears then as a whitish-blue puff of smoke that quickly merges with the air. Everyone has it, yet most of us live our whole lives without realizing it. That spirit or life force also has other names in other cultures, such as chi, qi, ki, mana, or prana. The word kundalini is most appropriate here, because it specifically refers to the ability to uncoil and travel up the spine. When this occurs, the ascending current blows open the energy vortexes, what we know as chakras, that are located along the spine. Like kundalini itself, chakras also belong to the subtle, non-physical body system we are all equipped with. When kundalini energy successfully moves through all seven of the chakras and exits through the crown chakra at the top of our heads and begins to circulate freely throughout the body, it ultimately brings about spiritual enlightenment. This is the mission of kundalini energy and the true mission of our lives. The process itself can take just several minutes or even less. If it happens spontaneously it is usually preceded by certain attitudes, behaviors, or life events that cause it to happen. It can also happen as a result of specific practices which can take months or years (or lifetimes) to eventually culminate in a full kundalini rising.

Another possibility for awakening kundalini is through contact with a guru, a person who had his/her own experience and is at all times aware of the multidimensional quality of existence and the true nature of being. A true guru possesses natural energy that can trigger the experience in others, if the recipient is ready for it.

The life-changing results of the self-realization experience need time and practice to stabilize. The length of time varies with each person and usually involves a lot of contemplation.

Every incident of realizing an enlightened state is a result of a full kundalini rising, but the stages of transition may not always be distinguishable with clarity. Depending on the individual, the current can move at different speeds. The power of a quick, forceful surge of kundalini and eruption of it through the crown chakra can make the different dimensions that were visited on the way seem like a whirlwind. There are many ways that an individual may come to have an experience and the passage of kundalini will vary from person to person, but the final result is the same for everybody.

MULTIDIMENSIONAL EXISTENCE

"What we perceive and project is a fusion of energy of all the chakras active in our system."

We are multidimensional beings. Throughout our lives, we experience and express the qualities of all seven chakras (dimensions), each of us in different proportion and to a different degree, depending on the condition of each chakra. What we perceive and project is a fusion of energy of all the chakras active in our system.

Modern civilization is mostly based on the activities of the first three chakras, while the other four are often suppressed and underdeveloped because so much of our energy and attention is spent dealing with the material world. Even though we all possess the instrument that can complete and enlighten us, the kundalini current and upper chakras are simply not known to play an important role in our lives. Over the centuries, churches and religions have held the monopoly on spiritual truths, and we've grown accustomed to a rather mechanical system of receiving those truths through a form of religious dogma. Dogma, translated into a set of rules, operates mostly in the realm of the third chakra and may restrict the depth of spiritual insight for the individual seeker of connection with God.

It is through upper-chakra vibrations that we can access incredible knowledge and benefit from the insights revealed by those levels of consciousness. The subtle body is visible in the dimension of the sixth chakra.

THE CHAKRA SYSTEM

"Each of us is a single unit of consciousness operating and experiencing life through the dimensions of chakras."

Chakras are commonly considered the energy centers in the body. During my kundalini process, without knowing anything about chakras beforehand, I experienced them as dimensions of perception. Here is what I mean: The vibration of each major chakra creates a specific kind of awareness in our consciousness. We cognize those different realms of existence and experience life in the ways that we do because of the energy each chakra harnesses. As kundalini moves through our body, it becomes clear that we are beings built out of our perceptions, including the perception of the material world. Hence, by the same token, we are not material beings in possession of a chakra system. Each of us is a single unit of consciousness operating and experiencing life through the dimensions of chakras.

These seven chakras have a hierarchy in our system, with the first being the lowest and the seventh being the highest. The lower chakras cannot give perspective to the higher ones, but the higher-chakra consciousness, united by freely flowing kundalini energy, can perceive the nature and state of all the lower ones. There are many, many more chakras than the seven that I list here. In fact, the whole universe is full of them, but to explain the complete kundalini rising and the phenomena of spiritual enlightenment, comprehension of the seven basic chakras and their functions is needed.

The whole world is spiritual. Everything that happens is projected by one single consciousness, the greatness of which we are not able to encompass with our minds, because our minds are limited. The mind we normally operate with is incapable of reaching all of the dimensions that express life. Under some circumstances some of us are able to perceive the dimensions of upper chakras. The kundalini travels up through those realms and allows for understanding the process of consciousness transcending from the individual to one and the same for all, The One. That opportunity for insight and transformation depends on the kundalini flow and on the state of the chakras. The kundalini resting in its seat between the first and second chakra can vary in strength; it may be strong in some individuals and weaker in others. Kundalini is an individual unit of consciousness, and life generating force. The latent kundalini is still our vitality and source of existence, but it is an existence shrouded in ignorance. Though we think of ourselves as the doers and creators of our own lives, we are more like zombies, stuck in our own stories without seeing that we are playing a role.

When kundalini awakens and travels up the spine, it cleans and revitalizes all the chakras. If it finds its way through all seven, one becomes enlightened.

WORDS

To explain the experience from my viewpoint, I need to make sure that certain words are understood as per my intent. The following are some distinctions to consider.

Emotions Versus Feelings

Emotions and feelings might have similar meanings, but here, I consider them to be two different occurrences. Emotions appear without thinking. We experience them spontaneously, organically. They come up and they are essentially simple. There is a whole scale of emotional tones, ranging from deep unhappiness to complete happiness. Their impact varies from very intense and overwhelming to very mild and barely distinguishable. Emotions are a direct expression of the second chakra. When they appear, they are not yet thought over.

Feelings are more complex and are based on the fusion of emotions and thoughts. The emotional energy finds mental reaction from the third chakra. Feelings are created by combining emotions and thoughts into belief systems that build our personalities and present to us the reality we experience. Their content is a combination of the second and third chakra energy.

Belief Versus Faith

Although these are often considered equivalent, belief assumes that something is or will be a certain way, without any need for a specific explanation as to why. It could be a suspicion, a gut feeling, a sentiment based on previous experiences, etc. Belief results from the merging of various factors strongly supported by the second chakra influence, personal emotional preference. While it is not always the case, belief can be destroyed by contradictory evidence.

Faith is a stance that belongs to the domain of the fourth chakra. It is even less provable than a belief, as it is more of an internal state that does not need to relate to any particular external circumstance. Faith is more powerful than belief, it is much more than a gut feeling. Like all fourth-chakra phenomena, it carries with it ethical qualities of full responsibility and devotion. Real faith cannot be destroyed by any evidence.

Mind Versus Intellect

Mind and intellect are often thought of as synonymous; however, in order to make a distinction between modes of reasoning, I need to assign the faculty of mind to the third-chakra dimension of perception and the faculty of intellect to the seventh. The third chakra relates to subjective knowledge, most often used in a utilitarian manner, revolving around strategic considerations such as going about daily tasks, learning new skills, figuring out plans, etc. It's motto is : "I know". The seventh-chakra mind is of pure intellectual nature. It reasons objectively, discerns abstract values, and is not concerned with strategies aimed at conquering problems. It is mainly occupied with observations and conclusions. It's motto is: "I witness". The method of the third-chakra mind is logical reasoning, used to design survival techniques and structural applications of all kinds of mental systems. The intellect I am referring to is used in philosophical thinking, contemplative studies, and any kind of abstract system not necessarily based on linear deduction.

The reason I make this distinction is because I could clearly observe mind and thought dissolving while the kundalini current moved through my third chakra. I recall some spiritual teachers' warning against thinking during meditation and tales about the mind being stopped and thoughts ceasing to exist. When it happened to me, what I was left with after the mind was gone was pure, unbiased intellect. It ceased to function only when the kundalini current blew through the seventh chakra.

Knowledge Versus Consciousness

Although knowledge and consciousness can be sometimes considered the same, for the sake of clarity, I make a very definite distinction between the two. Just as with the difference between mind and intellect, knowledge can be assigned to the attributes of the third chakra and consciousness to the seventh. Knowledge might expand consciousness and vice versa, but they are fundamentally different. Knowledge is what the mind uses for the being to function, prosper, and develop, while consciousness is an ability to discern a state of being. It is not based on knowledge but on the subtleties of awareness. Just like knowledge can vary from minimal to highly extensive, consciousness can also have many different levels.

Morals Versus Ethics

The difference between morals and ethics can be tricky, because there are many definitions of both. Moreover, in practice, they often overlap and are difficult to distinguish. For my purposes, I will use the following clarification: Morals are comprised of customs, habits formed in accordance with group judgment. They are agreed on by a group. Therefore, just like mind and knowledge, they are defined in the third chakra and become codes of proper behavior. Ethics are of an inner, individual nature and are brought about by the energy of the fourth chakra, the deep sense of goodness for all. Deeds that can be considered immoral in many cultures (like lying, for example), can be ethical from the standard of personal ethics (like lying to evade injustice for oneself or others). Ethical law is built on honesty, benevolence, truth, kindness, fairness, respect, generosity, helpfulness, and other beautiful, positive qualities relating to this noble realm of consciousness. Moral law varies depending on the culture of the group.

Religion Versus Spirituality

Religion is based on a system, devised by a person or a group in order to create a collective understanding and organize local beliefs. These beliefs can evolve over time and spread organically to a larger group, or, as we know well from history, beliefs can be enforced and can influence many generations that way. Although religion usually originates in the sixth chakra it is structured to serve a social group and it spreads control through the third chakra vibration. However, practicing religious rituals can help in opening and developing upper chakras, and this, in turn, can help to awaken kundalini.

Spirituality, is the natural tuning into an inner sense of divinity, our personal connection and communication with it. Spiritual insight originates in the seventh chakra and is manifested through all upper chakras. Practicing spirituality helps one achieve better balance between the lower and upper chakras, which leads to a more balanced life. Genuine and truthful spiritual practices help awaken kundalini.

CHAKRAS AS DIMENSIONS OF PERCEPTION

"Once the comprehension of chakras as dimensions of perception takes place, the realization of who we really are follows naturally."

Upon learning about chakras and the subtle body from external sources (the internet, books, other people, etc.), we create a visual understanding of the system. This imagery comes from ancient Hindu concepts developed from recorded kundalini rising experiences and the mystical tradition of spiritual enlightenment.

In the simplified form, basics of the subtle system are comprised of the following elements:

1. Kundalini energy;
2. Shushumna channel through which the kundalini energy flows up, once aroused;
3. Energy vortexes (the seven chakras).

As a result of my spontaneous experience, I was able to distinguish between specific stages in my inner travel and gain a clear and thorough understanding of what occurred. In the internal process of expanding consciousness, each stage had to do with a specific set of phenomena creating a world of its own. I refer to each stage or world as a dimension. Once the dwelling in one dimension was complete, I was lifted higher, into the next dimension. The nature of each dimension was thoroughly explored during the process.

In time, after I had read a couple basic books about chakras, I was able to draw an interesting comparison between the stages of my process and the nature of chakras as energy centers. I could identify the shifts of consciousness I experienced as movement of the kundalini current through the subsequent energy vortexes, the chakras. Once the comprehension of chakras as dimensions of perception takes place, the realization of who we really are follows naturally.

We all consist of the dimensions we perceive, but this statement needs more explanation. The concept of reality as an illusion might also be difficult to make sense of, because what we know as "reality" is the only real thing to us. However, it is possible to comprehend the truth of these concepts through the unfolding of the layered dimensions of perception during kundalini rising.

First Chakra – The First Dimension (Body and Material World)

We don't need to know anything about chakras, vortexes, or energy centers in the body to just *be.* In fact, our physical being has no awareness of any of that. The first dimension of perception is just that: physical being. We *are,* and there is a world around us. We breath, see, hear, smell, and touch, go through the bodily functions and that's all. There is no emotion, no thoughts. It just is you, grounded in the world around you. You physically manifest together with it. Can you find yourself just being, with no emotional attachments, no conclusions? It is the basic, raw state of being alive in a body.

Kundalini Energy Moving Through the First Chakra

Our consciousness in a dormant state is seated between the first and second chakra, in the sacrum area, at the bottom of the spine. In situations when we experience our physical existence in danger, kundalini awakens and kicks in as a survival instinct. It can be easily triggered to give us lots of physical energy that can also become a raw sexual energy. The physical manifestation of sexual arousal and orgasm belongs to the first chakra realm. If kundalini wants to move up the spine and encounters blocks in the second chakra, it can create hot or even painful areas in the lower body and around the spine. It can also stiffen and cause cramping in various areas of the body for a while.

Second Chakra – The Second Dimension (Emotions)

Although information about chakras can vary, depending on the source, the second chakra is usually connected with the emotional, sexual, and creative aspect of life. In accordance with my own experience and in my understanding, the second chakra is essentially the dimension of emotions. It perceives life as an emotion. Kundalini energy itself is sexual and creative in nature, with the sexual aspect manifesting more in the lower chakras and the creative one in higher.

The emotional world we experience can be very powerful. It is a highly individual world, resonating within a singular organism, but we can also connect emotionally with others and at times be emotionally interdependent. Emotions appear naturally as reactions to internal or external circumstances, and they can affect our lives tremendously in a good or bad way. We listen to them and we believe them. We identify with our emotions, often to the point of having difficulty separating ourselves from their impact.

Kundalini Energy Moving Through the Second Chakra

Kundalini energy can move up the spine through the second chakra when emotions are in a neutral state, what spiritual masters often deem *emptiness*, a non-emotional stage on the path to enlightenment. The energy can get stuck in the second chakra and cause emotional problems. The emotional component of the sexual act is released in the second chakra. Over all, due to proximity of the kundalini seat between the first and second chakra, and near the third chakra, our daily consciousness is continually under influence of the latent kundalini energy. We live, and although not fully awake, we experience our dormant spirit in a mixture of perceptions, mostly from the first three chakras.

Third Chakra – The Third Dimension (Mind)

The mind registers all that is going on within the physical and emotional world and makes decisions. It is geared to learn and to survive. Its strategies are logical. The mind, as a device, is much more powerful than any computer, yet like a computer, it is limited to one kind of reasoning, even when describing complex ideas. It employs linear thinking as it organizes knowledge. The mind operates continually and does not stop on its own. For most of us, whether we want it or not, the mind keeps going, and thoughts keep coming.

The material, emotional, and mental worlds belong to the first three chakras. The emotional world connects with the material world below and the mental world above and plays a decisive role in the nature of our outlook.

Those worlds of the first three chakras are already so rich and inexhaustible, so full of new experiences and emotions, so intricately structured, that the mind has a lot to think about all the time. The dimension of time (a faculty of third chakra realm) allows for creation of stories. The mind harbors these stories of specific events, memories from the past, and projections into future. Throughout our lives, we are completely immersed in those stories, as they seem to give us enough to think about and figure out, yet our imagination often fails to fathom measures we can't define through linear reasoning.

Kundalini Energy Moving Through the Third Chakra

The third chakra often presents a huge obstacle regarding kundalini rising. In my case I had to agree to commit suicide. My mind was not giving up. In truth, it didn't give up on its own. It was destroyed, won over. It never wanted to wave a white flag of surrender. My mind was beat after fighting ferociously, wrestled down, and annihilated by my full acceptance of my death.

If kundalini energy manages to enter the third chakra dimension, we can experience powerful bouts of clarity and immense joy. Levitation is also possible. If the mind truly surrenders its thought producing activity, kundalini energy will clear the third chakra on its way up. During that passage, one experiences transcendence of thoughts, and the constraints of ego get released. The visual sensations accompanying the later stages of transition are showers of gold speckles of light.

Sometimes, when the kundalini energy rises to the third chakra, but is unable to break through higher, one can become uncommonly knowledgeable on some subjects without ever studying them before.

Fourth Chakra – The Fourth Dimension (Love)

A lot has already been said about the upper chakras. It is important to know that they are realms of consciousness manifesting in different ways, allowing certain kinds of experiences to take place, and revealing expanded perceptions of life. They do not belong to the linear concept of rational thought, and they don't even take up time in the sense that we understand it. Such is the nature of the fourth chakra.

When our consciousness rises to the vibration of that dimension, we begin to feel the greatness and power of love.

Love changes our world into a home for the heart and brings goodness to all. The love of Jesus Christ has been healing the world for thousands of years, as has the love of other masters and saints. It is the same love that we all carry in our hearts, whether we are aware of it or not.

A person with a well-developed fourth chakra feels and cares not only for themselves but equally for others, including animals and plants. Such individuals naturally have high ethical standards and feel responsible for the world. For this reason, they often actively participate in creating a better world for others. The need to create love and peace in the world and working to do so manifests in various activities like the caring for and helping of disadvantaged people and animals, or of loving and protecting nature. Animals are just like us, and animal life is no less valuable than human life. Thus, the single most important thing everybody can to do today is to keep developing the fourth chakra, with the aim of feeling the power of that love and creating a loving environment for all life.

Kundalini Energy Moving Through the Fourth Chakra

The most beautiful experience of receiving and giving love takes place when kundalini energy moves through the dimension of the fourth chakra, because it is in this state that we realize that love exists eternally, beyond our mortal structures of the body, emotion, and mind. Upon that realization, we cross over from the mundane to sacred reality. Gentle swirls of ephemeral pinks and greens flowing into endless depths were there during the passage in my case.

Fifth Chakra – The Fifth Dimension (Connection and Sound)

An active fifth chakra is the domain of musicians and music lovers but also of those who express themselves through other forms of communication. It is expression, reception, and the exchange of energy through words, sound, music, psychic senses, etc. I think most of us can agree that music is a magical tool. It can help us emotionally, inspire us greatly, and change our lives for the better. It is the vibration contained in the harmony of sounds that affects us. Singers with beautiful voices draw their mesmerizing power from the rich well of the fifth chakra. Great writers and poets can express deep truths because their fifth-chakra energy facilitates that expression. We admire oratory talents because of the fifth chakra's embrace, which we feel when we are in the presence of people who are effective communicators. Many of us sing and play instruments because it makes us feel good. We often listen to music and have come to know that sound can heal.

Years ago, around 1981, I had an appointment that I did not want to miss, but I had been sick with a high fever, sore throat, runny nose, headache, and felt physically exhausted, and it looked like I would be stuck in bed for days. I had no knowledge of the healing properties of sound, but, instinctively, I sat down on the floor with my legs crossed and began to emit sound from the depth of my chest, all the way down through my core. It was the lowest sound I could make and I held that note for as long as I could. I continued to do this for over an hour. When I could not go on any longer, I crashed. The next day, I woke up feeling fine, and all the symptoms that I had been experiencing were gone. I was completely healed and I knew it was because of my unusual practice the previous evening.

Communication with angels, animal spirits, guides, deities, and all other beings, takes place in the fifth chakra realm. People with psychic abilities and other supernatural gifts have strong fifth chakras. This dimension is a timeless space, an ether, where all that has ever happened, is happening, or will happen is recorded, in detail. It is where all facts are known, held in the, invisible to the physical human eye, library of akashic records.

Kundalini Energy Moving Through the Fifth Chakra

Passage through the fifth chakra opens the world of connection. One can receive visits of other spirits and beings. Archangels, ascended masters and mystical teachers from other galaxies, times and worlds may offer greetings and transmit knowledge and support. Many beings are happy to communicate, teach, and help us. Music and various shades of blue may be present. If kundalini energy gets stuck in the fifth dimension and is unable to move up, a person can get stuck as well, and consider channeling other beings and their information as the ultimate truth. The powers and effects of those contacts can take over somebody's life and keep the person fanatically adhering to the received messages.

Sixth Chakra – The Sixth Dimension (Intuition and Vision)

The sixth chakra, also known as the third eye, is the realm of vision and intuition. Like the fifth, it is about information, but it is shared via visual or conceptual code, a language of symbols. Our beliefs and convictions about life beyond the material plane and all kinds of esoteric explanations about the creation and operation of the world come from this dimension. Our religious views are based on its messages as well. With this chakra active, prophecies were made and the Vedas, Bible, Torah, Koran, and many other sacred, and important scriptures were composed. All gods and systems of deities were created at this level of consciousness. Here, mysteries, in the form of a vision, are revealed through powerful prophetic messages, sacred symbols appear and become comprehensible. In the sixth-chakra vibration, we find otherworldly cosmologies and information about other beings, dimensions, and planets. Sacred geometry, astrology, numerology, Tarot cards, I Ching, and all divination systems are conceived by the dimension of this chakra.

Each religion claims to have the right god or gods and the proper kinds of practices. It is hard to convince one believer of a certain god to choose another form of worship, and transition into another system of beliefs. The messages from the sixth chakra come with certainty, resolution, and specificity, and cannot be easily altered. They speak on the level of the soul, beyond the material attributes of life and, people do perceive the visions to be real. The sixth chakra, when well-developed but still disconnected from the flow of energy between the chakras, can affect people in extreme ways. Religious fanatics or even great visionaries do not always have their chakras functioning in unison.

Visual artists get their inspiration from the sixth chakra. Again, one does not have to be enlightened to be a visionary, prophet, or artist; it simply requires an active, developed, and strong sixth chakra to receive the inspiration and information. My experience with the abstract dimension in 1988 was possible because of sudden expansion of the sixth chakra, triggered by years of intense painting and observation. These practices were often thought of by me as foolish, but I had high hopes of getting somewhere, of becoming a better artist.

Kundalini Energy Moving Through the Sixth Chakra

A lot can happen during passage through the sixth chakra, for it is a transit very rich in major realizations. We receive information, just like in the world of the fifth dimension, but this time, we comprehend it without the help of other beings: it occurs through our own inquiry into visions and symbols that appear during the passage. The soul realizes itself, and we become eternal beings. I write more about this part of the process in Chapter VI.

Kundalini energy, when stopped in the sixth dimension, may have a very strong effect on the individual. One can become convinced of being reincarnation of a known personality from the past, or of being chosen by god, goddess or deity to fulfill an incredible mission, maybe to start a new religion. The imagery and symbolism is taken literally as an order "from above" to perform some esoteric acts to influence and change the world.

Seventh Chakra – The Seventh Dimension (Pure Intellect)

Pure intellect is not the pragmatic mind we use to strategically navigate through life but, rather, it is the abstract mind, the acute awareness of what is, enabling us to make subtle discernments through observation. It is a witnessing awareness. Conclusions received through the seventh chakra are not used for a utilitarian purpose but, instead, allow the intellect to remain open for further unbiased contemplation. People with strong seventh chakras love thinking conceptually and love philosophy. Their favorite pastime is to think, and they like to resolve problems by thinking in abstract ways. They find freedom in thinking. Modern secular teachers of enlightenment encourage the development of this chakra, with primary focus on self-inquiry and contemplation. They inspire us to think in a nonjudgmental way. The spiritual truths and advice about life we seek to find most often come from the wealth of wisdom developed out of the seventh chakra.

Kundalini Energy Moving Through the Seventh Chakra

From the moment we enter the seventh chakra, our consciousness begins to fully integrate with the observed process, but it does not diminish the power of observation. The passage of kundalini through the chakras is from the start done in a form of self-inquiry. While the process is taking place, one asks questions and finds answers, which allow for the full comprehension of this vivid phenomenon. The last question and the last answer come right before one inevitably and naturally unites in bliss with the ultimate consciousness, also known as God.

POINTS OF TRANSCENDENCE

During the kundalini rising the pure, sublime current enters and clears each chakra from stagnant energy. That energy transcends and moves up together with the ascending kundalini.

Here are the points of transcendence of each chakra:

First: Loss of attachment to the body and focus on emotion.

Second: Movement away from emotion and arrival in a neutral space of emptiness.

Third: Surrender of the mind, the dissolution of all thoughts and ego, experience of boundless joy and omniscience.

Fourth: Receiving of grace and the fulfillment of sacred love.

Fifth: Acknowledgment from other beings.

Sixth: Seeing through the illusion of reality and experiencing the self-realization of the soul.

Seventh: Uniting in full awareness with God's consciousness.

CHAPTER V: PRACTICE

REASONS FOR PRACTICE

Nonreligious spiritual practice can begin for many reasons, but, in general, motivation comes from long term or short term goals. For some of us it will be the long term objective of self-realization, but for others it might start with simply improving personal life. Goals like healthy body, emotional balance, better focus, more success and happiness will become easier to accomplish as soon as we step on a conscious spiritual path. There are no prerequisites to begin and no conditions that could prevent it, but in order to progress most efficiently it is best to get help in establishing a path that optimally suits one's predispositions and circumstances. No matter what is going on in our lives, standing firmly on our own path will allow us to find our deepest, truest center from which to lead a happy and giving life.

As we get deeper into the practice the nature of our quest deepens as well. In this chapter I outline basic kinds of practice and conditions which are helpful on the path to self-realization.

CONSCIOUS AND SUBCONSCIOUS PRACTICE

"Expansion of consciousness and discovery of the inner structure of our psyche happens when we reach deeper into our own selves."

The inclination to engage in practices may stem from a conscious desire to work towards achieving a state of enlightenment, but in our modern, especially western, culture we are not taught to pursue such a goal. Many of us feel intuitively that some action must be taken to improve our state of being, even if the reason remains unclear. The practices done intuitively might be performed in order to satisfy personal needs, to overcome obstacles in order to progress towards any specific goal.

As the legend goes, Prince Siddhartha Gautama grew up sheltered from the harsh realities of life. As a young adult, the sight of poverty, illness, and death shocked him and made him choose a life of an ascetic, rejecting pleasure to understand the meaning of life. At the age of 29, he left the palace and his family, and vowed to achieve enlightenment through austere practices. At the age of 35, emaciated and worn out from exhaustion, he reached his goal.

Buddha's practices were conscious and deliberate. His path is as valid today as it was some 2,560 years ago. He overcame the same obstacles we all face when we try to realize the Self. He was asked to teach what he learned, but was reluctant at first, for he knew how highly sublime the transition into the enlightened state is and how difficult it is to grasp it from a lesson. Eventually, he was convinced to share his knowledge, and he created the system that we know as Buddhism. In time, many schools took on his teaching, and often those teachings became very intricate. Buddha's profound wisdom offers a moderate and calm approach in the direction to spiritual enlightenment. It is through practice of kindness and open heart that we progress on the path. Inside of each of us there is Buddha, the Enlightened One.

Ramana Maharshi had a spontaneous experience of enlightenment when he was only 16 years old. He described the moment his experience happened as something that followed a state of body death, which he admitted was induced by purposely imagining his death. He was frightened at first, but as soon as he conquered his fear the self-realization took place. Not long after that, he left home and spent the rest of his life contemplating the experience and, with time, he gathered many disciples. Like Buddha, he had no desire to teach, but he did so because so many requested it. His modern, virtually nonreligious teachings fall into the tradition of Advaita, an ancient school of non-duality between individual soul, Atman and creator, Brahman.

The experience can be evoked on purpose, as in the case of Buddha, or it can happen spontaneously. Either way, it is the same for everyone. We all have a subtle body and are capable of going through a complete kundalini rising experience.

When at the age of 16, at a library in Warsaw, I came upon the verse of Vedas about Atman and Brahman and experienced a surge of tremendous energy that lifted me up, my kundalini rose up to the third chakra and made me fly down the stairs and float over the street.

That was a prelude to what would follow years later when I had a complete kundalini rising experience.

My ardent spiritual practice was subconscious up until the time of my experience. First, I developed the skill of examining myself because of my upbringing. Then, to progress with my art, I learned to paint despite anything going on around me and regardless of how I felt. I did not think much of it; I just forced myself to do those things, based on a strong, intuitive conviction. Without knowing it, I was practicing self-inquiry and contemplation that led to further developments. Expansion of consciousness and discovery of the inner structure of our psyche happens when we reach deeper into our own selves. Self-knowledge and self-control are the basic, essential steps toward a deeper understanding of life. Engaging in these practices will naturally establish a solid spiritual path.

The beginners on a path need to stick to a routine of a focused practice that is limited to one activity at first. As one becomes more advanced, any activity can become a practice and eventually life turns into a conscious practice without effort, done with love and full, engaged presence. This is what we want, because we all want to live a meaningful life, where realization of our personal goals is serving all of life in the best possible way.

CONDITIONS FOR SPIRITUAL ENLIGHTENMENT

"Yogic lifestyle and nutrition, adapted to our modern circumstances, are most appropriate for a life on a conscious spiritual path."

As I just said, each of us is equipped with the system that can bring about self-realization. However, after I experienced my spontaneous process, I realized that getting to the destination was not only like finding a needle in a haystack but also like finding a way to go through the eye of that needle with my whole being. It is that miraculous! I later discovered that the conditions for full kundalini rising are the same for everyone who goes through it, that similar circumstances trigger the awakening of kundalini, and similar personal characteristics allow the energy to freely flow through all the chakras.

So many of us can experience sudden openings of the upper chakras by receiving downloads of valuable information, unexpected answers to our questions, or powerful suggestions that can bring important changes in our lives. We can feel guided by spirits or we might be startled by an insight that seems not to have come from our own viewpoint. Dreams and visions can be both illuminating and misleading, depending how we interpret what is happening. It is good to know the difference between a chakra opening on its own and together with the kundalini current moving through it. An independent opening of an upper chakra can be extremely powerful, but only in connection with the kundalini flowing through it do the visions and messages align with the rest of our perceptions. In many Buddhist traditions, little or no significance is given to visions because the emphasis is granted to the state where the visions transcend into the seventh chakra vibration, as a result of the kundalini travel.

Body

Stress on the body, which appears in the domain of first chakra, can cause kundalini to awaken spontaneously or intentionally. This stress is the result of various life-threatening experiences, perhaps an accident or purposeful neglect of the body, as the ascetics have practiced for millennia. In present-day western civilization, designed with material wellbeing in mind, this kind of behavior is unpopular. Why willingly subject your body to starvation or pain? The only and the well-justified reason is that it may cause kundalini to rise and culminate in enlightenment experience.

Near-death experiences (NDEs) often bring about a sudden kundalini rising. In NDEs, kundalini can also awaken as a life savior, manifesting as something stronger than any deadly situation to which one is subjected to. Such cases don't necessarily result in enlightenment; more often, it is the kundalini, our individual life force, leaving the body, only to re-enter it later and revive it.

A kundalini rising can be experienced on one's deathbed. In fact, it is more probable to experience spiritual enlightenment then, when one has achieved a sufficient degree of purity of mind. Making amends, clearing any lingering grudges, and finding peace makes it easier for kundalini to flow through all the chakras. The mind - (the third chakra) - will be less obstructed by thoughts and that way more ready to surrender.

Spiritual enlightenment is an experience beyond body's life and death, its realization exceeds time and the cycles of lives.

Yoga

Yoga is a practice that aims to help one on a journey to spiritual enlightenment through a variety of physical and meditative practices. That yoga has the potential to make us feel healthier and happier is just one of the natural, beneficial by-products of the practice. Another possible outcome of yoga is siddhis, special powers that some consider to be a proof of the enlightened state. In truth, one can become supernaturally gifted without being fully self-realized and vice versa - spiritual enlightenment does not have to mean possession of siddhis.

Yoga has become very popular all over the world, which is wonderful because, if exercised regularly, it has the potential to help many of us balance the chakras and awaken kundalini. It is very fortunate that these days so many more people are aware of the benefits of yoga and meditation, as those practices will result in more of us spiritually enlightened.

Yoga is a natural, intuitive practice, and it should be done with a direct, intuitive contact with higher consciousness as much as possible. Yogic lifestyle and nutrition, adapted to our modern circumstances, are most appropriate for a life on a conscious spiritual path.

Sex

Up until the day of my experience, sex and the complicated dynamics of sexual relationships presented a true mystery to me. There was always something inexplicable about it and I was very curious to find out why sexuality had so much power over people. In my own life, I intuitively considered sexual relationships to be sacred, but it did not seem that my partners or many people I knew felt that way. I found that quite confusing. My attitude was also influenced by observation of the subtlety and intensity of emotions connected with sexual love and their impact on a person's wellbeing and happiness. I wondered what it was about that precious and unique connection that can send us into the world of ecstasy and unbelievable happiness but can later evaporate into oblivion or bring us the worst emotional pain imaginable. I did not understand why such intense emotions could be evoked by sex, nor why it was so difficult to control them.

My experience revealed to me the true, profound meaning of sex and the connection between sex and spiritual enlightenment. Kundalini, our individual consciousness and life force, is survival, sexual and creative by nature. It affects the first, second and even the third chakra because of its proximity to them. Our sense of vitality comes from that place at the bottom of the spine, close to the sexual organs. When we are attracted to someone, and especially when we have sex with that person, kundalini gets awakened and we feel its true nature strongly. Joined in a mutually desired sexual act, our kundalini energies eagerly merge into one. The ecstasy and bliss are just the true nature of our divine source. Kundalini is dancing happily, feeling at home united with its own kind, awakened and vivid. Depending on the state of the chakras, the energy may enter the magnificence of higher dimensions and even culminate in enlightenment experience for one or both partners. During orgasm, kundalini energy is released physically and emotionally. Sexual arousal that does not result in orgasm can take kundalini higher, past the second chakra, because the unreleased energy can now push upward. Kundalini energy is tremendous and truly transforming, so powerful that if triggered when one or more chakras are blocked it can cause some physical, emotional, and mental problems. Sex is the gate that can lead to true liberation in the most profound meaning of the word; however, to experience that gate open, other requirements (chakras letting the kundalini energy pass through) must be met first. Although some form of a sexual act is often present before kundalini rising takes place, it does not always need to be so.

For the realization of the eternal soul, gender is not important. Any individual seeking self-realization does not need to be concerned with gender as a beneficial or detrimental factor in the process. Gods and goddesses exist in the realm of the sixth chakra, but the ultimate consciousness has no such attributes. That consciousness has no form, which means that the realization of consciousness is beyond our human form as well.

Emotions

A powerful emotional state can bring a person close to death, such as in the cases of severe depression with suicide attempts. In those dire states, one does not use their given vitality to embrace the world outside; rather, that person is closed off. This is why spontaneous experiences of kundalini rising can start with the depressive state, because in emotional pain, most attention and energy is spent on dealing with the problem. Just to be clear: this is not an invitation for someone to develop depression or a serious emotional problem, but a note, that such situations are an opportunity for tremendous growth. The intuitive search for spiritual enlightenment often starts with a problem that affects us emotionally. Recognition of the emotional state is the first step in the kundalini rising process and first step on a path to spiritual growth. If one can acknowledge the emotion and then arrive at a neutral state, one gives space for the healing and renewing flow of kundalini energy to enter. The ability to get into the neutral state of emptiness is a condition of awareness that kundalini requires to pass through the second chakra. The condition that has a chance to trigger the awakening of kundalini does not need to begin with a negative emotion, but the emotion should be intense enough so using the power of will and focus will make a noticeable difference. Naturally, when taken by a positive emotion, we don't want to bother with stopping it or changing into a neutral state, so it is mostly in times of hardship that the kundalini energy spontaneously wakes up.

It is important to note that very, very few of us can innately and effortlessly remain focused to such a degree that kundalini can find a way to flow up, but consistent practice can make it happen.

Even though prayers and mantras address the dominions of upper chakras, they also can help with retaining the state of neutral emotions and focused mind.

Mind

I received incredible insight as my kundalini energy flowed through the third chakra. It began with images, but then memories connected to the images were recalled with great accuracy, as if those moments were actually happening again. The train of thought presented itself perfectly, taken directly from the time track of my life story. We all have the ability to recall our past experiences, even if we believe that most of our memories have been lost. During my experience, my mind could answer questions that it had been unable to answer before. My mind analyzed all the thoughts and brought them to the present in their full context: complete, concluded, and resolved. Once those thoughts arrived at the present time they vanished, but their energy remained - it became a result-oriented, faultless reasoning. My mind was then ready to operate on a present time level, cleared of the clutter of all the content creating thoughts, allowing for an astounding measure of analytical activity.

Although the actual phenomenon happens on its own, there is a condition that can gradually lead to it. This is where the effects of previous self-inquiry and the practice of focusing the mind prove indispensable. Conquering one's own mind is the hardest part of the whole process, the biggest obstacle to self-realization. It is a process that needs to take place naturally, after some preparations. Learning about yourself can take time. Observation, focus of vision, meditation, contemplation, and self-inquiry are the methods that will induce the transition from a subjective mind to a fully objective, universal mind.

It is well worth knowing, that one does not have to have a brilliant and powerful mind in order to experience the third chakra transit. What matters is that the mind is mature and the self-knowledge and the ability to focus is sufficient.

While performing those practices, the mind will not know when it is ready for surrender. In fact, it is likely to protest and negate your efforts. It can pretend other states of consciousness and make a fool out of you, if you let it. It will probably continue to circle back to the same stubborn dismal statements, but be confident that the proper practice will ready it anyway. This is why it is important to never give up, to keep going. If the practice is done without any renunciation of the external world, the effort can take many years, because new issues and new situations will engage the mind, new groups of thoughts will form and connect with the older groups and concepts, continually stirring up new stories. By suggesting to renounce the external world, I do not mean that it must be done by seeking solitude in a cave until enlightenment is achieved, even though this is a path followed by Buddha himself. You could simply establish an agreement with yourself, to determine that self-inquiry is your priority. From then on, it will be up to you to make appropriate choices and refrain, as much as possible, from things that absorb your attention. For these reasons, a minimal diet without indulgence is suggested, as is a modest life without distraction. It might seem that work and family could be insurmountable distractions, but in those circumstances, one can practice mindfulness, a practice that will eventually lead to more opportunities for peaceful self-inquiry. The most important thing is to start immediately, regardless of circumstances. In time, external conditions will align themselves with your inner focus.

Upper Chakras

The fourth, fifth, sixth, and seventh chakras are, usually, less developed than the first three. This is because most of mankind considers material success the only real, pressing necessity and thinks of other values as optional. Contrary to that belief, the truth is that we need to use the consciousness of the upper dimensions to evolve and transform into more beneficial beings. By cultivation of upper dimensions of perception we can become less troubled, destructive and ignorant. While practices helping to clear the lower chakras can seem like an effort, especially in the initial stages, work on upper chakras is often fun.

Kundalini energy can stop at any blocked, weak, or underdeveloped chakra and cause health problems, or it will simply retreat to its place at the bottom of the spine. Sometimes, a strong current can jump over the blocked chakra and continue to move through the ones above, but such instances can end in illness, emotional imbalance, and delusional states, not in self-realization. We can prevent these adverse effects by cultivating and nurturing the upper chakras. Life tends to improve dramatically when we do. People whose upper chakras are more developed and active are more predisposed to experience a full kundalini rising. Artists in all media tend to have more developed upper chakras, because they consistently engage them in their creative endeavors. People with strong, well-developed upper chakras are often on a conscious spiritual path. These individuals have probably experienced too many instances of signs from the upper chakras to ignore them as insignificant. Messages like this appear in the form of inspirations, support and guidance, visionary revelations, sudden profound insights, and moments of exceptional clarity and understanding.

Heart

Jesus Christ personified the fourth chakra in his teachings. The joy, happiness and devotion of love, given and received, is the value of the open fourth chakra. Many of us who have big hearts and are naturally loving and giving, already have our fourth chakras open and strong. For the kundalini current to fully enter the fourth chakra, however, we need to experience a "receiving of grace". This means we will be taken under the loving care of the Presence, whose existence we will become fully aware of at that moment. Jesus taught love and bestowed grace on others because he received it first. So taught Buddha and other great teachers, like the contemporary beloved Dalai Lama. At the moment of receiving love and falling in love with the Presence who reaches out to us, we realize that it is our dream come true, the love we've always wanted and dreamt about, even if we thought ourselves naïve for desiring unconditional love. Perhaps you thought that kind of love didn't even exist or that if it did, it had to be found in another human. When we receive grace, we see and feel that love does exist everywhere, all the time, and there is no doubt about it, because of the transformation it brings. The practical conclusion is very simple: The cultivation of love keeps the fourth chakra open and makes it grow. Everyone needs to practice active, loving thoughtfulness and wish all others well. It often means taking care of others before we take care of ourselves. Love, ethics, and genuine care for the whole of life needs be practiced daily. Love is not a weakness or a utopian dream; on the contrary, it is a phenomenon of higher consciousness, of a dimension of the fourth chakra, and there is no enlightened state without full awareness and continuous practice of love. The Sanskrit word "bhakti" means practice through love, faith and devotion, aspects of the fourth chakra. In loving environment everything thrives.

Energy Healing

Energy healing is also done through the connection with the upper chakras' vibration. The power of energy healing depends on the strength of the upper chakras of the healer. The most compelling factor in energy healing is the vibration of the fourth chakra. Love heals.

Passion and Dedication

Anything that is not easy to achieve requires passion and dedication to fuel the effort necessary to overcome the obstacles we find on the way to the goal. We all know this, but it is good to remember that passion and dedication to a cause does not have to feel especially rational, logical, or perfectly balanced with other interests or activities. It is even recommended that one pursues goals with undivided devotion. It is good to have a burning desire and be able to feel a strong and demanding sense of purpose.

The Arts

The best way to cultivate the fifth and sixth chakras is through the arts. Playing instruments, singing, and listening to music help to develop the fifth chakra. Conscious listening to the voices we hear and feeling the energy of communication is an important practice. We become more sensitive to the nuances in the sounds, learn to listen, and feel the vibration of sound more and more clearly. Sounds and communication are all around us all the time, but it is the refinement of our listening and performing practices which cultivates that dimension. Some of us are naturally gifted, but practice is advisable for everyone, talented or not. Sensitivity to the messages we receive and care for what we communicate to others are ways to bring attention to the magical realm of the fifth chakra.

The sixth chakra develops through observation. Although it might seem there is nothing to be gained from staring at one spot for hours a day, or, as in my case, staring at paintings for years, this practice brings about very valuable results. The general cultivation of visual arts, either by being an artist or by loving art, develops the sixth dimension. It also enhances imagination and visionary intuition. All arts develop a sense of harmony and aesthetics, values created by upper-chakras' consciousness. Regardless of what the art is, involvement in it leads to the opening of the fifth and sixth dimensions and allows for the development of the process of creation. That process is the same as the performance of a magical ritual. The third eye is the eye of the sixth chakra, it is the eye that receives a vision.

Ritual

Ritual is a combination of all upper-chakra dynamics. It is put together in order to call a desired result into manifestation. Rituals are inherent in all religions, but they can be equally or even more powerful when performed in a nonreligious way by individuals or groups. Rituals combine faith, communication, intuition, vision, and philosophy. All these concepts strengthen the upper chakras and expand our consciousness. Performing a ritual helps the kundalini current in its passage through the upper chakras. Rituals deal with symbols and archetypes, derived from the sixth chakra, and performance, derived from the fifth. Faith is vested in the outcome of the ritual and comes from the fourth chakra. The sacred meaning of the ritual is created with the seventh-chakra perception.

Dance

Movement invigorates slumbering kundalini and, like yoga, dance can be a fantastic spiritual practice. All forms of dance are great for energizing kundalini, while the dance as an art form, and especially as a ritual, can help opening up all of the upper chakras.

Self-inquiry

"Self-inquiry is the single most important act that leads to spiritual enlightenment."

While "bhakti" is performed from the heart center, another kind of practice is done through self-inquiry, which involves contemplation, discernment and other attributes of the seventh chakra. Some of us love the pursuit of abstract thought, but for others, it is not easy to even begin thinking that way. This is why it is advised to ease into the self-inquiry process with the third chakra self-knowledge study, to find out about yourself through simple observation and analysis. The advanced self-inquiry is led from the seventh chakra and consists of deep contemplation on the subject of one's being.

Self-inquiry is the single most important act that leads to spiritual enlightenment. When kundalini energy travels through the third chakra it frees our mind and uncovers its pure analytical power to solve any problem. The inquisitive power of the third chakra mind is absorbed into the finely discerning seventh chakra intellect, ready to conclude on the basis of pure witnessing and comprehension. This is the secret of the kundalini passage through the upper chakras: the self-inquiry process develops naturally and brings one to ask the right questions intuitively. The right answers are given naturally, until unity with the source is reached. Therefore practice of contemplation of self-inquiry questions and answers is essential to self-realization.

Sat-sang

In Sanskrit, as we discussed before, this word refers to a coming together of those seeking spiritual truth. It is good to receive support from and give support to others who are on their own spiritual paths. Reading this book can be considered a sat-sang, as can communicating with a friend who practices any kind of meditation or yoga, as long as you support one another in your spiritual practices. Getting together with others for meditation or discussion about spiritual issues comprises a sat-sang. The path to enlightenment is solitary, especially in the later stages, but converging with likeminded individuals can be very helpful.

THE SEVEN STEPS TAKEN ON A
CONSCIOUS SPIRITUAL PATH

Step 1 - Is to give up attachment to the material world. We do have bodies, but we are not just bodies and we do not need to identify our being with our body. It does not mean neglect of the body and material world, but simply keeping in mind that the material world is just a small part of a meaningful existence, not all of it .

Step 2 - Is to give up identification with our emotions and seek a neutral space of emptiness.

Step 3 - Is to seek freedom from thoughts. This can be done gradually, in various ways, like meditation, focusing mind on an object, and engaging in the self knowledge (elementary stage of self-inquiry).

Step 4 - Is to cultivate by practice the qualities of the fourth chakra, like love, compassion and benevolence.

Step 5 - Is to seek and practice communication for the purpose of development and growth.

Step 6 - Is to practice intuition and develop visual understanding.

Step 7 - Is contemplation and advanced self-inquiry.

CHAPTER VI: PATH TO THE ENLIGHTENED STATE

HIERARCHY OF DIMENSIONS

"Learning how to tap into the incredible wealth of the upper chakras is important for our survival and prosperity."

During the kundalini rising process, the hierarchy of the dimensions becomes clear. We can observe how each of the worlds, the dimensions of perception, transcends into the higher one while leaving the chakras below open and aligned. First-chakra consciousness is that of life on the physical plane. For each of us, the experience of the first chakra is limited to our senses, our bodies, and our current surroundings. The emotions we feel about this experience are naturally subjective and belong to a world of many gradients and delicate overtones that are always prone to change. Emotions accompany our every move, and even if we don't realize it, they supervise our physical reality like monitors. They control our lives by suggesting preferences to do one thing over another.

Above the physical and emotional is a mental sphere, one that oversees both realms below and makes sense of them. It builds complex mental structures that include the knowledge about the material and emotional worlds put together, along with all the elements of mind power, including will, memory, strategy, planning, calculation, execution, and judgment. The third chakra often tries to exert control, for that is one of its assigned tasks. In the case of controlling the physical, emotional, and itself (the mental dimension), its work is necessary to create a functioning system, both on the individual plane and in society and the environment. It's an activity regarded as common sense, providing logical, practical solutions to all kinds of problems.

The energy of the upper chakras is not malleable and controllable by the mind we use today. At this point of human evolution, very few people can control their chakras. Learning how to tap into the incredible wealth of the upper chakras is important for our survival and prosperity. Cultivating and developing the upper chakras will invite the kundalini energy to ascend in peace, unite all the dimensions with its flow and bring spiritual enlightenment to each of us.

The power of the fourth chakra is enormous. This dimension invariably and continually bestows grace on the whole world. It reaches everywhere and encompasses all that is material, emotional, and mental at all times. It brings love and it heals. It can be naturally open in some of us, can suddenly open under some circumstances, or the kundalini will burst it open if it travels up.

By the time our up-flowing kundalini reaches the fifth chakra, the mind is already free from personal issues and can analyze and resolve any problem successfully. We feel loved, open, and loving. Tuning into the fifth dimension, we discover we are not alone. The universe is full of communicating energy and we can receive much guidance and support from many sources. The fifth chakra links elements of the same frequency vibrations, creates harmonies, arranges serendipitous situations, and allows us to participate in the world of magic. This is a world where everything is possible, far beyond the material world we are so stubbornly anchored in. All communications that ever take place are registered in this realm, in a timeless fashion.

Encompassing these five dimensions is the sixth chakra, where our human stories are explained through myths, archetypes and symbols. In this dimension, truths are revealed and mysteries are solved. The whole of the world, all minds and all systems of thought, can be reached here, presenting themselves in telling visions. The realization about the illusion of our mundane reality takes place. Thereafter, still in the realm of the sixth chakra, the soul self-realizes. Also in this dimension, one can attain deity status.

SIXTH CHAKRA TRANSIT

"Once seeing past illusion, consciousness can transcend further, into the magnificence of eternal soul."

There is a sequence of insights that accompany expansion of consciousness during the sixth-chakra transit. Although the themes of the passage might be different for each individual, the sequence remains of the same character, as it is comprised of proper questions and answers leading directly to deeper expansion and understanding.

1. Vision is presented and comprehended

In the instance of the sixth chakra opening without kundalini passing through, one can receive a vision but will not necessarily comprehend it. With kundalini awake and present, one can decipher the mystery contained in the vision. The vision I received during that passage, the matrix of creation, is one others have experienced as well, and their accounts have been the same or very close to mine.

2. Subsequent revelations

Conclusions are reached by grasping the sense of vision that leads to further discoveries and propels us on the path to self-realization. As a result of these discoveries, one can comprehend the illusion of reality we experience during our lifetimes. The explanation of this process is challenging because it takes place in a mind free from the doubts and restrictions of the third chakra, not the mind full of thoughts and mental structures. All the analytical thinking present during the discovery process, is also accompanied by visual thinking, which is incomparably faster and begins with careful observation of the vision and continues throughout. The linear mind of the third chakra analyzes precisely the results of visual comprehension.

As I said above, each person who experiences this process may have a different vision and method of understanding it, but the results and conclusions will be the same:

a) Everything going on in our lives is conceived in the domain of the sixth chakra

The lives we live, our personal narratives, are already projected in a field beyond the reach of our senses. We live through that projection often worrying how to survive, to keep up, and to make something good happen in our lives. There is no need for it, as all that takes place in life has already been designed. To the third chakra system of operation - linear reasoning, this statement appears crazy and unfounded but, as I said earlier, the seven dimensions we perceive do not operate according to the same principles. The agreement we have about the physical reality and how to deal with it is based on the logic of the third chakra perception and this is the universal reference we are considering when making decisions, individually or in group. Anything that is not common sense or is not scientifically proven seems rather dubious. However, one can thoroughly understand the sixth-chakra vision if one's mind is free from the ego paradigm, which binds together energies of the first three chakras and limits our perceptions to the physical, emotional and mental. We can grasp the paradox of time and no time simultaneously while kundalini flows from the first through the sixth chakra and from the perspective of that dimension. For me, perceiving that our lives were incubated on a grid, with each of us representing a code of information animated through an individual life story, was a startling, mind-blowing finding. To learn instantly afterwards, that together with our lives, another concept (time) is also conceived in the matrix of creation and serves a purpose in observing the continuity in our lives, was another amazing discovery. It is because of the previous experience of my thoughts vanishing and realizing myself as a free mind, able to comprehend and resolve any problem, I could follow the development of those realizations precisely. The clarity of the illusion is unmistakable, and one finds a way to see through it at that moment. Once seeing past illusion, consciousness can transcend further, into the magnificence of eternal soul.

b) Consciousness is eternal and exists beyond any number of eons of lifetimes and life stories

This statement comes as a clear and unequivocal conclusion, based on the results of the inquiry.

c) The soul self-realizes

One finds one's true identity as an eternal being and embraces all aspects of life in all six dimensions as a stage of evolution created by the soul itself. Self-realization equals the comprehension that one consciously creates one's own life on the soul level.

d) All is created by thought

Our individual consciousness, with kundalini current transiting smoothly from the region of the first through the sixth dimension, becomes clearly aware that everything that exists, either in a material or non-material state, is gathered in the realm of the sixth chakra in a conceptual form. Some of those concepts materialize and we can experience their manifestations, but others remain as thoughts.

3. Soul self-inquiry.

The soul, being a creation of and passing through the sixth chakra, sees itself but does not yet see the source of the energy it has ben receiving.

Just like at the beginning of the sixth-dimension transit, the self-inquiry process develops in a natural way, through questions and answers. The soul can ask any question and find an answer to it. In my case the question I felt compelled to ask was, "What creates life?" While I did not know that it would be the last question I could ask, receiving the answer catapulted my consciousness into final stages of spiritual enlightenment.

ABOUT OUR SOULS

"Your soul is your master."

Soul exists in the sixth chakra realm. Your soul is your master. It creates each person and gives us the challenges that we own until they can be transcended. Which means that we create ourselves and in that way we are completely responsible for our lives. Through self-inquiry each soul can accomplish its mission more efficiently.

THE FINAL STAGES OF KUNDALINI RISING

"At the point of the kundalini current moving through the crown chakra, all the realities, concepts, ideas, and thoughts vanish in transcendence."

My question "What creates life?" brought a loud and lucid answer that exploded in full brightness. I could perceive the thoughts shooting spontaneously from the source of infinite intelligence, which now felt very close. The thoughts were powered by an inexhaustible force of inspiration, so tremendous that no words are sufficient to describe it. I realized, that, in truth, the whole world is being created spontaneously, anew in each moment, with all the physical manifestations and all the systems of perceptions of higher chakras. Our common, daily consciousness (a coiled, slumbering kundalini) is most aware of the physical, emotional, and mental dimensions, while others reveal themselves in glimpses, ephemerally and mysteriously, except when kundalini rises and flows. As kundalini rises, it visits all the dimensions (chakras) necessary for the experience of the truth of who we are. In one of the early stages of the sixth-chakra journey, the illusion of reality becomes unmasked. Thereafter, in the later stages, one consciously awakens as an immortal being existing beyond that illusion. That being comes to full self-realization and comprehends its role in the creation of the world. This is the place of final discernment that all of life is a mirage and exists only as ever-changing potential!

Inspiration creates the world. At the moment the full recognition takes place, the seventh chakra bursts open. One quickly merges with all that exists.

One remains consciously united in a state of bliss and ultimate awareness and creation of everything, a state that is indescribable. This is where the soul merges with the divine, where the self-realized individual abides in nirvana, moksha, mukti, liberation, satori, or, enlightenment. Even though there are no thoughts in this state, the witnessing intellect, the Self, is present in full awareness.

In most of Hindu traditions, the soul (Atman) exists. In Buddhist understanding, there is no soul. From the viewpoint of my experience, this conflict of opinion may be caused by the fact that only in the last stage of kundalini rising does it become clear that nothing really exists, that there is no world, no ego, and no soul. When the kundalini current passes through the sixth chakra, we realize the eternal soul, because it exists then. That kind of consciousness of the eternal soul (Atman) is more real than the consciousness of the ego, because at that moment, it contains all six dimensions in proper interdependence. Since the stage of self-realization is a discernible state of full competence, the eternal soul can communicate and express its presence independently of time and space, until it becomes one with all.

At the point of the kundalini current moving through the crown chakra, all the realities, concepts, ideas, and thoughts vanish in transcendence. In their wake, a sense of ecstasy, fulfillment, and bliss arises. The full awareness has no concepts or words.

From other accounts of the final stages of the enlightenment process it becomes obvious that the speed and force with which kundalini breaks through the chakras can be extremely fast and powerful. The goal is reached, but, as I mentioned earlier, either some parts or simply most of the rapid, explosive journey may be impossible to describe in detail.

FROM EGO TO SELF-REALIZATION

"We stick to the ego mentality because we are not yet taught how to transcend it, and most of us don't even try."

Each of us varies in the intensity and power of the kundalini current we experience, as well as in the strength and development of each of the seven chakras. The most common combination is that the first three chakras are stronger and more developed than the upper ones. People who are successful in business professions usually have a more developed third chakra, but overall, the shape of our common reality is determined by how those three chakras relate to each other and to the chakras of others. We are multidimensional, spiritual beings, but we are dominated by material, emotional, and mental values. The reason the material world governs us is not because it is of paramount importance but because our upper chakras are inactive, our kundalini asleep. Power and money are often in the hands of people who think the world is ruled by power and money, and that's the third chakra perception world to which we have been subjecting ourselves for thousands of years. Conflicts between people of different religions, territorial aggression, the horrors of war, famine and economic crises, lack of sufficient education to help us evolve into better beings, humans abusing each other, harming animals... that list goes on. The ego prevails, and this is the meaning of the word *samsara*. We stick to the ego mentality because we are not yet taught how to transcend it, and most of us don't even try. We consider our situation normal and from the ego perspective, a human being is selfish and destructive because it needs to win the fight for survival against other selfish and destructive human beings. It is extremely hard to find a person who, without practice, has strong lower and upper chakras with the kundalini energy flowing between them naturally. Even when a person achieves that state, at some point, further practice is needed to maintain it. As Ramana

Maharshi said, "No one succeeds without effort. Those who succeed owe their success to perseverance."

Whether unexpected, sudden and spontaneous or purposefully sought and achieved through deliberate practices, enlightened state is realized by following the same pattern: Awakened kundalini travels up from the bottom of the spine, blows open all seven chakras, clears them, and leaves them full of pure consciousness.

Once kundalini reaches the seventh chakra in the proper sequence, without omitting any chakra on the way, time will be needed to create unwavering state of enlightenment. In the final, stable stage, kundalini will naturally settle in its evolved seat in the heart chakra.

THE SEAT IN THE HEART

"Once settled, the state of being in the heart is easy because of the love one feels and gives."

It might take time to bring kundalini to the heart. For years after my experience, I felt vibrating energy traveling all over my body. The tiny chakras everywhere, 108 of them, as observed by the masters, open and clear of any stagnant energy. It can take time for our systems to go through the full transformation. Because of the engagement in the worldly activities, the practice of bringing kundalini to the seat of the heart can sometimes be as challenging as the initial awakening and ascendance through the chakras. Staying in the heart means feeling love and loving without any exceptions or judgements. It means being a medium for love to flow through. Once settled, the state of being in the heart is easy because of the love one feels and gives.

People, who after the full kundalini rising experience have their consciousness reside permanently in the heart chakra are the enlightened masters who can heal and enlighten others just by being. Their energy is very powerful. Teachers who possess this energy can reach those who are close to awakening and help them with the final step, regardless of distance in time and space.

POETRY AND PHILOSOPHY OF SPIRITUAL ENLIGHTENMENT

"Through inner work on ourselves we can advance as beings and our troubles, and the troubles of the rest of the world will keep diminishing as a result."

When our upper chakras open, we often get glimpses or even full insights into different, inspiring worlds. As I already mentioned, it is mainly through the practice of unconditional love and of arts that these chakras can develop and stay open for longer periods of time, revealing to us the sacred truths of higher dimensions of perception. Music and visual arts can touch us powerfully and the sense of connecting with creative energy can overcome us, but the words of great poets and philosophers can lift us up to a place of a, perhaps, more accurate, verbally confirmed conceptual understanding.

We can read and listen to profound spiritual truths and develop our own seventh dimension, so we experience our own glimpses of magic and deep insights and feel life as a much more profound and incredible experience. We can come up with our own words of wisdom, but for most of us there is a need to train the lower chakras, as that is mostly where the lingering energy creates blocks. That stagnant energy prohibits the yearning to ascend kundalini from flowing freely and fulfilling its mission of uniting energy of all the chakras, and bringing on the spiritual enlightenment.

Understanding that we are all creation and creators of the same eternal consciousness lies within us all the time, but the mind always tries to obscure it with ideas, replace it with rules, argue that it knows better by upstaging our sublime intuition with scientific proof, and then it still keeps on doubting. Science and the progress it offers is great, helpful and inspiring, but science is still just the external knowledge that belongs to the external world. To solve our problems, rather than perpetuate them or create new ones, we need to look inside our own being and deepen that insight with practice.

The path inward might seem impossible to find at first among the jungle of feelings and thoughts we've been accumulating, but with a machete of single-mindedness, we can cut out the trail and travel inward. In doing so, each of us will be led to the inexhaustible source of happiness, light, power and inspiration, to unity with the eternal conscious creation at every moment. Through inner work on ourselves we can advance as beings and our troubles, and the troubles of the rest of the world will keep diminishing as a result. This is what the one consciousness we all are is calling for.

CHAPTER VII: QUESTIONS AND ANSWERS

The following questions and answers have been collected from various group and individual sessions. I noticed that these types of questions are most frequently asked, and therefore, could be most relevant and helpful to you.

Q: You asked me to find my emotion and step out of it to find the neutral space. I have not succeeded at stepping out of myself. How do I do that?

A: We identify with our emotions a lot. When we are experiencing something that affects us emotionally, we often find ourselves at the mercy of that emotion. Our whole story seems to justify how we feel. However, the very empowering truth is that we really *can* exist without the impact of that emotion. It is possible to reach that state with practice, but that practice may not always bring immediate results. Practice anyway. Start by identifying the emotion and then learn to use your mind to enter a neutral, non-emotional state. Some additional preparation in the form of self-knowledge exercises and meditation may be necessary.

Q: I get inspired to meditate and do yoga, but after a while, I get bored with the whole routine. I am not even sure I'm seeing any results. Should I continue?

A: Most important is your agreement with yourself

about the nature of your practice. You should establish it according to your own natural predispositions. It may be something different from meditation or yoga, or maybe there are other obstacles you must identify and remove so meditation and yoga will work better for you.

Q: I grew up Catholic. Although I do not practice Catholicism and don't attend church, my parents do. When I started to pay attention to my spiritual views aside from religion, I realized that, in spite of the non-religious approach, I find myself going back to the story of Jesus. It seems I understand it better now and approve of the Catholic religion even more than before. How do you explain that?

A: Based on what we know of his life, Jesus has become an archetype of the spiritual hero in the most extreme and unforgettable way. In that sense, he evokes the deep spiritual truths and a lot of good, healing energy comes from that. On the other hand, his placement is within a patriarchal religious system; therefore, that dogma can obscure our innate spark of consciousness, because it creates rules that set limits, and boundaries that prevent expansion.

Q: I have been practicing meditation and self-inquiry according to your suggestions. I think I've made progress in finding out about myself and taking more control of my life. The problem is that everything goes well until I have to deal with my divorce and all the problems connected with it. I fall apart then, and my meditation gets disrupted by my emotions. I thought it would dissipate with time, but is has not.

A: The very obstacle on your way to a peaceful life has shown itself in meditation. This is already a progression. It means that you now know what you should focus on. It is the crucial first step to identify the main emotion that is causing the problem. The second step is to engage your mind in guarding your freedom from unwanted emotions. In time your mind will become clear and your unwanted emotions will disappear. This is the core of practice.

Q: How do you know the experience you had was the same as that experienced by Buddha?

A: This question does not have an easy answer, because the proper answer becomes clear only after the experience. Before that, it can only be seen as an argument, a topic of discussion, or simply blind acceptance of the fact. I can tell you what I know, but confirmation will only come from your own experience. There is no need for anyone to simply take my word for it. If what I do helps you with anything, that is already great.

Q: I was given a mantra to meditate with years ago. I used that off and on, but then I found another method, along with another teacher. It seems that after fifteen years of various practices, I should be doing better, but I am not sure. Sometimes I feel that the more I reach for new ways of gaining balance and peace in my life, the more disillusioned and lost I become.

> A: The *way* you apply the practice in your life is more important than what it consists of. The key to a successful spiritual practice is not to expect specific or promised results but to do the practice itself as if it is unrelated to those results. It doesn't matter how many schools you go to, mantras you learn, or teachers you have. It is about focusing on your own, inner path, before anything else.

Q: When I try self-inquiry, nothing seems to come to me. Why is that?

A: Self-inquiry is not something everybody can dive into right away. It is often important to start with the know-yourself challenge first, which is simply learning about your own life as you already know it but giving yourself a new account of it. Self-inquiry is the next step.

Q: Your experience happened many years ago. How much of it is valid in your everyday life today?

> A: The experience led to a recognition of a condition beyond life and death. A condition that never goes away. It is valid in every aspect of my life and it affirms its validity in my communications with others.

Q: I would like to practice more, but I don't have time. Fifteen minutes a day doesn't seem like enough for me to see any results.

A: Think of that 15 minutes as the most important part of your day. Dedicate yourself to the process, and you will see results. You will also find more time for it, even if now it seems impossible. Things will change!

Q: I am interested in the multidimensionality of our beings, and I'd like to know more about the mysteries of life, but I really don't want to practice. Won't it expand my consciousness if I put some effort into just learning about these things?

A: Learning new things will expand your consciousness, for sure, but think of it as reading a fitness book versus actually performing the exercises explained within it. When you just read, you are likely to absorb just a small part of the message. On the other hand, if you do the exercises, you have a chance to absorb incomparably more and truly own your new knowledge in practice.

Q: I have changed my life, and I like it. I find yoga very helpful in keeping me at peace and more focused. If I add a proper diet and self-inquiry, what results can I expect within the next six months?

A: I like your plan. Practice will produce results, but your expectations can actually become obstacles to

your success. Expectations are mental structures created in the third chakra dimension, so if you focus too
much on them, your mind will fool you and even present fake results, which is confusing and disappointing.
Rather, engage in the process of your practice and let
it take you to the results. Then, those results will be
real.

Q: Would you recommend cannabis or maybe other drugs
as help on a spiritual path?

A: Cannabis can temporarily affect upper chakras by
opening them. We can receive support and information from those realms and it can feel great and maybe even seem useful on our path. However, the purpose of self-realization is to be free. You don't want to
create a practice of dependence on any consciousness
altering substances. Your true self, the kundalini waiting to be awakened, contains all of your dreams come
true and more. Go straight to that source, in yourself,
and do the work yourself, so you can own your results.

Q: Question: How do I interpret my sexuality in the context
of my spiritual practice? What is the connection?

A: Awareness that kundalini is sexual in nature is an
important aspect of conscious spirituality. In the lower chakras, especially in the second one, kundalini can
manifest strongly. In upper chakras it gets sublimated
and takes on the vibration of upper dimensions. Basi-

cally, practices on kundalini and on all the chakras that you would do by yourself, you can also do with your partner. Practice self-knowledge together and learn about each other. It is usually the focus on the second, third and fourth dimension that will keep improving the personal relationship. The more conscious your approach to the relationship, the more sexual union can naturally become a sacred ritual leading to spiritual enlightenment.

Q: I've heard you mention a couple of times that there is no need to worry, because "it is all happening by itself, anyway". I don't get it. You mean if I just sit in one place and do nothing then all that I need to do will get done by itself? You know it is not true. I would get in awful trouble very quickly that way (laugh).

A: Try it. Try to sit in one place. At first you will find out that you can't sit in one place for a long time. You will soon get up and do something, even if you don't want to do anything, even just to go to the bathroom, to eat or lie down and sleep. It is because you are an integral part of the whole that is happening by itself. If you keep on trying to sit in one place, if you manage to sit long enough, while practicing resistance to the external stimuli, you will eventually grasp the actual state in which we all exist. It is a state of being a witness and a conscious co-creator of the perpetually appearing and passing, impermanent phenomena. It is a state of bliss. With this realization you will understand exactly what I mean by saying that it is all happening by itself.

Q: A friend of mine brought me to you, but I don't really have existential problems. I am successful in my career, love what I do, have a nice family. I am a vegetarian because I don't want to kill animals, I help everybody whenever I can and I understand life enough not to lament and despair over problems, but solve them. If I have any problems it would be lack of time to accomplish more, or maybe just to have more free time. Any other issues are also practical, more immediate; they come up and I look for a way to fix them, but I don't feel the need for a transformational experience to enjoy life. I guess my question is, can any of your teachings be useful to me at all?

A: Regardless in what state and stage of life each of us is in (feeling great, good, fair, or bad, successful, accomplished or a loser, etc), practice is needed. Start with a few minutes a day and gradually get up to maybe 15 minutes a day, since your time is limited, of the second and third chakra practice. Acknowledge the leading emotion, whatever it is, then move away from it while focusing on your breath. The neutral emotional state, when you reach it, is particular and feels like a vacuum, neither good or bad. You should be able to notice very soon what that seemingly inconsequential practice brings to your daily life. You need to see it by yourself.

Q: Is there a difference between *self-realized and spiritually enlightened?*

A: These terms are often used interchangeably. Spiritual enlightenment is used more in Buddhist tradition, while self-realization is a term taken from other mystical schools, mostly Hindu. They basically refer to the same thing, as each describes the final stages of kundalini rising process. At first, the person finds themselves being an immortal soul. That state can be already considered self-realization, because one has finally consciously realized the self-creation of their own soul. But the process still continues when the self-realized soul (Atman), upon a specific consideration, merges with the light (Brahman, God), and becomes enlightened. This is why I prefer to use spiritual enlightenment to signify the last possible describable stage of the process. To realize the Self in the last stage of the kundalini rising is to merge with all there is in full awareness and consciously participate in live creation of everything that is, not only of the self-created soul. One can argue that there is no spiritual enlightenment without self-realization, but there is a stage when one is self-realized, but not yet enlightened.

For information about offered sessions, programs and events please visit: www.moniquerebelle.com or email to info@moniquerebelle.com